THE CABIN

THE CABIN

Inspiration
for the
Classic American
Getaway

DALE MULFINGER AND **SUSAN E. DAVIS**

The Taunton Press

The Taunton Press
Inspiration for hands-on living™

The Taunton Press, Inc., 63 South Main Street, PO Box 5506, Newtown, CT 06470-5506
e-mail: tp@taunton.com

Distributed by Publishers Group West

DESIGN AND LAYOUT: Lori Wendin

ILLUSTRATOR: Martha Garstang Hill

COVER PHOTOGRAPHERS: Milroy and McAleer Photography (front cover);
davidduncanlivingston.com (back cover: top left; spine; front flap: top);
Randy O'Rourke (back cover: top right); Charles Register (back cover:
bottom right); Rob Karosis (front flap: bottom; back flap: top)

LIBRARY OF CONGRESS CATALOGING-IN-PUBLICATION DATA:
Mulfinger, Dale, 1943-
    The cabin : inspiration for the classic American getaway / Dale Mulfinger and Susan E. Davis.
        p. cm.
    ISBN 1-56158-392-8 hardcover
    ISBN 1-56158-644-7 paperback
    1. Log cabins--United States. 2. Vacation homes--United States. I. Davis, Susan E.
(Susan Elizabeth), 1942- II. Title.
NA8470 .M78 2001
728.7'2'0973--dc21   2001023571

Printed in Singapore
10 9 8 7 6 5 4 3 2 1

The Cabin was originally published in hardcover in 2001 by The Taunton Press, Inc.

I dedicate this book to my grandchildren: Olivia, Quinn, and Lewis. May their generation enjoy cabins as well.—D.M.

To my brother, Thom; sister-in-law, Nancy; and their kids Andy and Sarah, Meg and Dave, and Ian and Julia. Here's to all the good times we shared in cabins on Cape Cod, at Leech Lake on Mom and Dad's 50th anniversary, and in the years to come. —S.E.D.

Acknowledgments

THE CREATION OF THIS BOOK has been a thoroughly collaborative venture. The authors, who live many miles apart (Dale in Minneapolis and Susan in New York City), relied on many early-morning phone calls, countless FedEx packages, and zillions of e-mails, as well as three intense work sessions in Minneapolis, to create this book. But, though separated by distance and disciplines (Dale, architecture and Susan, writing), we found we had a similar vision and sensibility about cabins. Sharing that made the process easy and fun.

We certainly couldn't have worked together as harmoniously and efficiently without the able assistance of Jan, Dale's wife. She spent hours patiently shuttling our copy back and forth via the Internet and entrusted Susan with her computer during work sessions. Jan also kept us healthy and happy by whipping up several delicious gourmet meals when Susan worked late. We couldn't have done it without you, Jan!

And we couldn't have done it without our editor, Steve Culpepper, who initiated the concept for the book, introduced us to each other, and encouraged us along the way. Thanks, Steve, for all your input and enthusiasm. We also want to thank everyone at The Taunton Press who contributed to the book, especially Steve's assistant editor, Carol Kasper, who helped us keep track of so many pieces of data. And we appreciate all the Taunton photographers, including David Livingston, whose wonderful pictures contribute so much to this book.

Of course, we are very grateful to all the homeowners whose cabins we considered for this book, but we are especially appreciative of the final 37 who agreed to let us feature their cabins. We couldn't have produced this exciting volume without your help and cooperation. Thank you for being so generous with your private retreats.

D.M.: Thanks to the students of my research class at the Department of Architecture, University of Minnesota, in particular, Kristen Paulsen and Dan Wallace. Thanks to friends and colleagues who gave me leads and to several national magazines, particularly *Sunset,* for informing both the public and us of great cabins. And thanks to Susan for helping to translate, from photos and drawings into words, the ideas about cabins.

S.E.D.: Thanks to Thom and Nancy for letting me stay with them during the Minneapolis work sessions, for driving me to see the Mulfinger and Rapson cabins, and for all your support. Thank you, Dale, for tracking down so many of the cabins in this book, for promoting my interest in and knowledge of architecture, for pitching in when I had computer and scheduling problems, and for lending me your special "cabinologist" mug when I needed inspiration. You're the best!

Contents

Introduction

BACK TO NATURE. SOLITUDE. Simplicity. Escape. Intimacy. Self-sufficiency. Romance. Refuge. Resourcefulness. Nostalgia. These are the feelings that cabins evoke, and they're at the root of my passion for this elemental building form.

I'm not sure when my love of cabins started. My Minnesota farm family never took vacations, but it was during my childhood that I became interested in basic, elemental structures like chicken coops and corncribs. It wasn't until college that I entered my first cabin. Its do-it-yourself, hands-on quality—lots of sweat and ingenuity—

immediately appealed to me. After I wrote *The Architecture of Edwin Lundie* (Minnesota Historical Society Press, 1995), which identified me with cabins, I began to get a few commissions. But I felt I needed to know more about the building type, so I started researching cabins with my students at the University of Minnesota. That led to articles about cabins in *Mpls./St. Paul* magazine, and then a local talk-radio personality, Joe Souceray, who had seen the articles introduced me as a "cabinologist." The title stuck.

"Le Porch" (on p. 166) was the first cabin I built for my family. My wife, Jan, and I are now building a lake cabin near the Canadian border. I've built four other cabins on that lake, four more are under construction, and several more are on the drawing boards. Though I've visited hundreds of cabins and designed scores of them, the cabin as a building type continues to excite me.

When The Taunton Press contacted Susan and me about writing this book, we gleefully accepted the challenge of searching for a sampling of the most intriguing cabins in North America. Our goal was to find cabins that interested us as places we wanted to retreat to. We searched for variety, regional and geographic differences, and design attitude, old and new. We initially established a goal of 50 cabins, none larger than 1,200 sq. ft. We rejected tree houses, sheep wagons, yurts, and teepees. We sidestepped lake homes with master bedroom suites and catering kitchens. And we reluctantly rejected some great spaces that exceeded our size limit. There are thousands of wonderfully inviting cabins we have yet to see. However, we feel confident that the 37 cabins in this book show a great diversity, a breadth of design, and the best that cabin living has to offer.

For the Love of Cabins

THE KNOTTY PINE INTERIOR of this rustic getaway captures our collective memory of the quintessential cabin. Hand-made furniture adds to its comfortable charm.

A CABIN SITTING GENTLY IN A PASTORAL LANDSCAPE embodies our primitive sense of shelter. A fresh snowfall adds to the solitude of this simple retreat.

W E ALL HAVE A CABIN MEMORY. Or a cabin dream. The little place where the family vacationed when we were young. Tiny cot-filled cabins at summer camp. The honeymoon cabin. The cabin we built when the kids were small—or the cabin we want to build when the kids are grown. We remember our own cabins, or we recall some shared national memory, like Lincoln's or Thoreau's cabin.

The truth is, in function—if not always in form—modern cabins are no different from those historical ones, except that people today usually don't live in their cabins full-time; we escape to them instead. Retreating to these tight, safe quarters in the woods, by the water, in the mountains gives us the pleasures of an older, slower lifestyle. Usually it's just for a weekend, though some of us manage to escape there for good.

The Randolphs made such an escape. After working hard and raising four children, they dreamed of retiring to a cabin on Lake Superior. Though neither had a particular style in mind, they spent weekends driving the back roads, looking for the perfect place. All they knew was that they

A CABIN CAN BE SITED TO BLEND WITH NATURE. Painted the color of tree bark and integrated with the tree line at the edge of a lake, this cabin is an understated presence in the landscape.

wanted a cabin that felt right for them, nestled in the woods with a view of the lake. They'd know it when they saw it, they told the Realtor. Finally, they were shown the "little knotty pine thing," and both said "sold" just minutes after the Realtor opened the door.

Now they start each morning, weather permitting, sipping coffee on the porch that overlooks the lake. A few feet away, waves crash on the rocks, geese skim over the vastness of water. What will the day bring? Splitting wood, baking a pie, taking a walk before supper. The most exciting local news, gathered on shopping trips to the nearby town, is of a wolf spotted in the woods or a deer swimming in the lake. On blustery days, the stone fireplace is stoked, and their little cabin seems to huddle around them. They're supremely grateful for their cabin life.

The Randolphs are typical of year-round cabin folk, but they're no different from people who use their cabins only when the mood strikes. Cabins appeal to people in all the basic stages of life: baby boomers who want a weekend getaway; families who need an affordable vacation home; single people seeking a country haven; and

retirees who want something permanent, but scaled down, in fine surroundings.

Anybody who's attracted to the cabin's modest lifestyle can build one from scratch just about anywhere, usually without disturbing the land around it. Cabins may be fashioned from an existing structure—say, a forgotten hut or an abandoned garage. Or they can be built at home—in the garage, basement, or backyard—and assembled on-site in pieces, as time permits. And all it requires is a bit of land in a beautiful place and the stuff to build it—a modest amount of material and a generous supply of ingenuity and imagination.

The Special Qualities of Cabins

Though they may look very different from north to south, mountain to field, there's something special about cabins, something that sets them apart from small houses. It's often only a matter of the feeling a cabin evokes. While there are no clearly defined rules about what makes a cabin unique, there are several characteristics that make a cabin a cabin. Although all cabins may not share all of the following features, each cabin conveys the very essence of a shared spirit.

The site is chosen for its natural beauty. A cabin offers easy access to the outdoors, both through exterior rooms and through great views from inside. A cabin adds to the land, never dominating it.

A cabin provides simple, basic shelter. It isn't fancy. It doesn't try to make a social statement, as houses often do. A small, efficient floor plan is all it needs.

Overlapping activities take place within the compact quarters. Thus a cabin promotes companionship and community spirit.

Everybody feels at home right away. A cabin's furnishings are simple, often treasured family hand-me-downs. Its sleeping lofts, tucked under the eaves, evoke memories of childhood. Its fireplace or woodstove provides physical and emotional warmth.

Choose a Beautiful Setting

Every place offers its own pleasures: watching the sun rise over the Atlantic, fishing in the mountain river that rushes past the door, or taking in the mirrored serenity of a deep-woods lake. All you need is the desire to be part of it. Fortunately, a lot of places can still be called cabin country—anywhere a person can retreat into unspoiled beauty and seclusion. And today's cabins can be built without destroying the natural beauty of the site.

Architect Mark Simon was charged with protecting an ecologically sensitive floodplain bordering on a wildlife preserve when constructing the Marsh Pavilion (on p. 178) on the Atlantic coast. That's why he had the cabin

NESTLED BY SPRUCE ON THE SIDE OF A GLEN, this cabin respects and preserves the majesty of its Colorado mountain site. The sounds of the roaring stream fill this traditional cabin with nature's music.

prebuilt and assembled off-site. The planning paid off. The land remains a haven teaming with wildlife.

Respecting the environment is only one part of the unspoken code of cabin building. Another part is that no matter where it's built and whatever it's built of, a cabin should enhance the landscape, not overpower it. The best cabins don't overwhelm the land, they blend into it. That's why cabins often seem as if they grew out of their site, like the one that sits in the midst of Washington's Methow Valley (on p. 142). It appears as integral to the 3-acre site as the native pines and mounds of scruffy sagebrush. Situated to take full advantage of both the prevailing breezes and the expansive mountain views, the cabin appears to float on the landscape.

BUILDING WITH NATURE   The site itself often determines a cabin's design. A Colorado mountaintop will inspire a different design than the shores of a Minnesota lake, the Louisiana backwoods, or the stark Utah desert. Ron Mason's cabin in the Colorado Rockies (on p. 192) has a huge open deck that's just made for watching the clouds roll across the mountains or the Arkansas River

THE CONTOURS OF THE LAND can influence a cabin's structure and character. This rustic cabin cascades down a hillside in small-scale increments.

GREAT PLACES IN A SITE NEED TO BE PRESERVED as outdoor rooms. This setting is the perfect spot to while away time with a good book or to watch a sunset with a friend.

BASIC SHAPES CAN
REFLECT THEIR SITE.
Here, a gable roof
resembles the moun-
taintops beyond.
Located in an open
landscape, this form
harmonizes with
distant images.

rush by only a few yards away. A Minnesota cabin has to be snug, dry, and cozy like a heavy winter coat—yet it also needs to open up in the summer so it doesn't store heat.

The Atkinson cabin in Louisiana (on p. 214) has a variety of deck spaces, which encourage the owners to sit outside at any time of the day. The decks aren't just attached to the cabin, they're a central feature. Inspired by the traditional dogtrot design (a cabin type favored in the South because of its openness), the two rooms are separated by a roofed but open deck. You have to step outside to go from living area to sleeping area. But that's what a cabin is all about—connecting with the outdoors.

OPENING UP   No matter where they're built, most cabins have decks, patios, and porches, either enclosed or open. These kinds of exterior rooms make it easy for people to live comfortably out-of-doors in season. Like the Mulfinger cabin (on p. 166) that sits on the edge of a small, spring-fed lake in the Wisconsin woods. Thanks to its two screened sides, the cabin provides adequate shelter during a rainstorm but promotes constant interaction with the elements.

Sometimes an outdoor room is created by the land itself, when a cabin is in a glen, clearing, or meadow. The simple, solid cabin that sits all by itself in Washington's spectacular Methow Valley (on p. 142) makes a strong statement as it connects majestically with the land and sky around it. Its roof could even be mistaken for one of the foothills of the Cascade Mountains in the distance.

Simple, No-Frills Shelter

European settlers were the first to build cabins in North America—simple cubes or rectangles constructed much as their ancestors had built them. The size of available trees and the length and weight of a log that two people could carry determined the modest size of the earliest cabins, usually one room wide and two rooms deep. Gently pitched roofs were easy to build, shed rain and snow, and provided enough room upstairs for a loft, where children slept or the family's few possessions were stored.

These primitive cabins had only a doorway, often covered with skins, and no windows at all. It was well into the nineteenth century before cabins got even tiny windows, which in those days were paned with greased paper to repel water. Eventually, wooden shutters were added to provide nighttime insulation and defense against winter. Later, double-hung or hinged windows let in fresh air. Things really haven't changed all that much when it comes to building cabins. A cabin still offers protection from the wind, rain, cold, and heat and, like the log cabins of yore, provides at least minimal creature comforts.

A SIMPLE TRADITIONAL STRUCTURE OF MODEST SIZE hugs the rugged shoreline. A contrasting color articulates the cabin's domain and blends with the winter landscape after the leaves have fallen.

TREES CAN MOVE INDOORS as stair rails and benches, reflecting their origins while recording the craftsman's tools that produced them.

THIS 1,100-SQ.-FT., TWO-STORY CABIN creates intimate interior space. Its compact size allows birds and rustling leaves to merge with the friendly banter of close family and friends.

BUILDING BASIC   The cube or rectangle is still the most common cabin form. Construction continues to be basic, using readily available materials, including sticks and stones and, more recently, plywood or tin. The structure is formed from 2x4s or logs and has a sloping roof.

Many cabins start as a weekend project in a city garage. After the parts are built, they're hauled to the wilderness in the back of a pickup truck. As opposed to the earliest cabins, whose size was determined by the weight of a log that two people could carry, the size of these modern piece-built cabins is dictated by the dimensions of a truck—though the weight of the parts is still limited to what two people can carry.

And as in the past, nothing about today's cabins needs to be formal or stylish. City rules don't apply. Unlike a house built under the watchful eyes of the local building inspector and mortgage lender, remote cabins often need to meet only local zoning and septic system codes. Simple details add texture and design. Homemade doors, window boxes, and stair railings are added bits of personality.

AFFORDABILITY AND RESOURCEFULNESS   Part of the fascination with building a modern cabin is that it's relatively easy and affordable. No huge investment of time or money is needed. Deane Hillbrand spent weekends over the course of a year handcrafting a 12-ft. by 18-ft. log cabin on Minnesota's Sturgeon Lake (on p. 24) for a final cost of $2,000—including the cost of a log cabin–building class. But Deane was fortunate; his grandparents gave him the land on their property, and he was able to

THIS 400-SQ.-FT. TRADITIONAL CABIN is lifted above the landscape and parked gently on the slope. Pier footings help anchor the structure while preserving the tree roots.

MODEST COLORFUL BUILDINGS CAN BE PLANTED IN THE LANDSCAPE like oversize flowers. Follies, like the guest house on the left (by James Stageberg), have a rich tradition in garden design, where they are used to adorn the view.

use dead elm trees and—when they ran out—aspen, balsam, and pine as the logs.

Not every aspiring cabin owner is eager to build from scratch. A realistic alternative is to buy a ready-made kit. It took Michael Mortenson and two friends a 3-week vacation to assemble the shell of his cabin on Washington State's Whidbey Island (on p. 130).

Small Is Just Enough

Size is important when defining a cabin. (The cabins featured here are smaller than 1,200 sq. ft.) Though retreats of several hundred square feet are tiny by today's home-building standards, anything over 1,200 sq. ft. is more like a cottage, lake home, or lodge than a cabin.

The wealthy elite who built summer fishing camps in the Adirondacks in the late nineteenth century chose to downplay the size of their huge camps by calling them "cabins." But that's a misuse of the word, which comes from medieval English and describes a small room on a

BUILT-INS CREATE COZY SPACES in cabins, where furniture, architecture, and structure intertwine. Wood gives instant warmth to any interior.

ship (that's still the first meaning in modern dictionaries). So when Viola says in Shakespeare's *Twelfth Night,* "Make me a willow Cabine at your gate," she's referring to a tiny hut fashioned of twigs and boughs. Today's cabins, more often than not, still fit that description.

Even the smallest cabin in this book—James Stageberg's at 210 sq. ft. (on p. 204)—has all the standard amenities, including kitchenette and bathroom. Other small cabins, like the Mulfinger cabin (on p. 166) and the Ryan/Meyer cabin (on p. 232), don't include indoor plumbing. But taking a walk to the outhouse is part of the cabin tradition.

SMALL MEANS FLEXIBLE   Because cabins are small, they have to be flexible—and versatility is the key. Built-in storage and furniture are obvious solutions. A window seat can hold firewood or wet boots, board games or frying pans. Drawers, a pantry, or firewood may be tucked underneath the stairs. A closet might double as both attic and cellar. All that's needed is some thought about the most efficient way to make use of the space.

CLOSE QUARTERS BRING PEOPLE TOGETHER
Efficient use of space has a powerful effect on people in the cabin. Tight quarters promote closeness and companionship. That's why cabins are important places for people to bond with other people—not just with nature.

LORE IS IMPORTANT TO A CABIN. It can represent a region, family connections, or maybe just mythology.

Living in close quarters has another surprising effect: It promotes informality. Nobody expects you to show the same social graces in a cabin that you do around the citified dining table at home. With your nearest neighbor 20 miles away, who would notice—or care? Common courtesies, however, may be more important than ever in these small spaces.

Home Is Where the Cabin Is

Because they are often passed down through families, cabins tend to collect bits and pieces from everybody who came before. Wooden floors record the scuffs and scratches of generations. Drawers may bulge with things that nobody felt comfortable throwing away. And little caches of stuff collected over decades by cabin children

CABINS TEND TO COLLECT FAMILY TREA-SURES and mementos that chronicle the lore of these special retreats. Time and accumulation guide the design motif.

PORCHES EXTEND THE LIVING SPACE, as in this rustic cabin, and are a source of joy during warm-weather months.

show up now and then: a pile of shapely little stones, a folio of snakeskin, a steel toy. Grownups leave their mark, too: a hand-pieced quilt, old fishing rods mounted by the door like artwork, furniture that reached its prime back when only women wore earrings. These treasured objects give each cabin its own special personality.

Furniture is just as likely to be early attic as Ralph Lauren. There are no demands for high style, unless that's what the owner wants. The bare light bulb fits just fine with the secondhand refrigerator. The coffeepot and iron skillet are preferred kitchen utensils, and blenders and food processors just don't seem like necessities. Storage is often exposed, so dishes, pots and pans, plaid shirts, hats, and walking sticks become decoration.

No matter where the cabin is or what else is in it, nothing spells home more powerfully than a hearth. Frank Lloyd Wright built a huge stone fireplace in his tiny Seth Peterson cabin in Wisconsin (on p. 226). Wright believed that people instinctively need to huddle together around a fire—that, as the fire warms us physically, it satisfies deeper needs. Fireplaces can take as many forms as cabins. Observe the different types of stone fireplaces in this book—everything from the rough-hewn hearth in the Flippin cabin (on p. 80) to the sculptural one in the Winton cabin (on p. 208).

Shapes, Styles, and Materials

To most people, the word *cabin* conjures up images of a log cabin, thanks to the little log home's picture-postcard place

LOCAL MATERIALS MAKE A CABIN PARTICULAR TO ITS PLACE. Here sponge rock and oak logs were used to create a hearth that's connected to the landscape beyond.

THE MEMORY OF A VERMONT COUNTRY SCHOOL has been preserved with this cabin transformation. The former school's new life promotes its lore for a few more generations.

in our history. But now the field of choices is much wider. Cabins come in nearly an infinite variety of shapes and styles, and they're built from an amazing array of materials, including sticks, stones, sheet metal, and even glass.

Based loosely on shape, design, age, and material, we think about cabins in four general styles: rustic, transformed, traditional, and modern. Stylistically, these varieties often overlap, but we find it helpful to categorize cabins in this way. The 37 cabins we bring together in this book offer inspiration for anybody who wants a modest, efficient place where he or she can forget the demands of city life and indulge, instead, in the good life.

The Rustic

Rustic cabins, often resembling the classic log cabin, are a rich part of our cultural legacy. Their designs were often passed down through the generations via apprenticeships, word of mouth, or old pattern books. Timeless, no matter when they were built, their primitive style and nostalgic character speak to us in a familiar, comfortable language that's easy to understand.

Their floor plans, based on a simple rectangle, reflect the straightforward logic of the carpenter. The 14-ft. by 16-ft. log cabin the Schwob family built in Minnesota (on p. 54) is typical of a rustic cabin. Each corner of its one room accommodates a different household function—cooking, heating, reading, and doing projects.

Rustic cabins aren't limited to one room. The Solberg cabin in Wisconsin (on p. 36), with six rooms and two porches, is also rustic. Its rooms are a series of simple rectangles, and several have exposed studs. Electricity and plumbing are also exposed, making them easy to repair; and storage of most items is visible—on nails, hooks, or shelves anchored between studs.

Like other important historical markers, the presence of rustic cabins enriches our cultural landscape.

EVEN MOBILE UNITS LIKE SHEEP WAGONS CAN BE TRANSFORMED into cabins, though such small spaces often need exterior rooms. The lean-to at the left is a great place to drink coffee on summer mornings and to store firewood in winter.

The Transformed

Recycling older structures is commonplace in many cultures. It validates our sense of ethics, ecology, and occasionally pragmatics. Why throw out perfectly good logs from an old barn when they can be salvaged, recut, and reused? Bernard Flippin did just that when he built a cabin in the Blue Ridge Mountains of Virginia (on p. 80). After dismantling a late-nineteenth-century tobacco barn in North Carolina, Bernard used the chestnut and oak logs to build an 18-ft. by 19-ft. cabin in the yard behind his brick ranch house in Fancy Gap.

Transforming an older structure takes imagination and effort. You have to envision the possibilities and then find a way to make them happen. That's what it took to restore an unused garage only yards from the beach on Massachusetts's Cape Cod (on p. 86). The location was ideal, but the two couples who bought the place wanted a vacation home that slept six. Because their budget was limited—$20,000 including architectural fees—they opted to renovate the garage rather than tear it down.

The transformed cabin offers something special: instantaneous lore, an essential characteristic of cabin life. Patrick Hanley was inspired by history when he rescued a falling-down shack in a Montana ghost town. Once called Maiden, the town had been the hub of Montana's gold-mining industry and one of its largest communities in the 1880s. But it was abandoned when the gold ran out. Hanley decided to save one of Maiden's original buildings, a tiny cabin owned by the saloon keeper, Tom Kerr (on p. 92). Hanley had local contractor Bud Barta disassemble the cabin, construct a new foundation, and reassemble the building with a new porch, while preserving as much of its authentic character as possible.

The Traditional

As traditions are passed along, they evolve. Tried-and-true, the simple rectangular building with a gable roof is the most typical form cabins take. Yet their basic building parts may include the most up-to-date technology, and their interior layouts may vary from the usual one room.

CULTURAL CONNECTIONS LEND INDIVIDUALITY and character to a cabin. The Swedish stencil motif on the wall reflects the owner's ancestry.

Like our common language, traditional cabins feature local dialects along with modern idioms.

Just compare the Shelden cabin in the Montana wilderness (on p. 148) to the Chapman cabin on the Maine coast (on p. 184). Architect Jeff Shelden wanted something small, romantic, and characteristic of the Rocky Mountains, so he designed his cabin to resemble a traditional forest ranger's station—a lookout tower much like the ones in which his dad worked as a forester many years before. Plus, Jeff's wife, Lois, wanted the cabin to have plenty of light. Building up was also the best way to take advantage of the site near the bottom of a narrow 113-acre canyon called Alpine Gulch. Windows on all four sides of the tower provide expansive vistas up and down the canyon. Plain white wainscoting on the interior is a traditional finish. The cabin does have a few modern touches, however: Electricity comes from solar cells, and there's a hot tub outside.

The tradition of Maine boathouses is reflected in the Chapman cabin, built as a guest cabin over boat storage. The exterior is covered with traditional New England wood shingles, and the plan is a simple rectangle with a gable roof and double-hung windows. The exposed wood framing on the interior is common to summer cabins that don't require insulation. Such a casual, unfinished place makes the experience of living in it casual as well, like walking around without shoes on a summer day. The tradition of exposed frames is common to cabins but rare in houses, where interior finishes are as decorative and comparatively formal as a shirt and tie.

The Modern

Who says you can't experiment with a cabin? The Yaukey cabin in Nova Scotia (on p. 220) proves there are plenty of innovative ways to capture the essence of a cabin using new means of construction, adapted forms, and new ways of defining space. Evolved from boat-building traditions, the Yaukey design features a large hull of space to be lived in as casually as an urban loft.

Even logs can be used in new ways, as in the Winton cabin on Lake Superior (on p. 208). Though Nick Winton wanted the cabin he designed for his parents to fit in with the other cabins on Lake Superior, he also wanted to experiment. So he nestled the two-story cabin against a hillside and shaped the end facing the lake like a ship's prow made entirely of glass. By placing the prow behind a

LARGE EXPANSES OF GLASS IN MODERN FORMS can also suggest basic shelter, where nature is let inside and rooms feel engaged with the outdoors.

huge, two-story stone fireplace, the architect lit up the interior with views of the lake.

Often delight, whimsy, and daring drive the builder, designer, and/or owner to do something that's never been done quite that way before, which is what inspired architect Ralph Rapson's all-glass cabin in Wisconsin (on p. 238). While glass has been common in high-rise office towers since the 1950s, Rapson applied similar thinking to his retreat in the pastoral Wisconsin countryside. Because he didn't want the view blocked, the cabin's walls grew by the stacking of conventional sliding glass doors until Rapson had an all-glass cube. To give rigidity to the tenuous glass, a

ONE OF THE MOST FAMOUS CABINS IN AMERICA was built by Henry David Thoreau in Concord, Massachusetts (a replica is shown here). Living there alone from March 1845 to September 1847, Thoreau was inspired to write *Walden*.

MUCH CABIN LIFE TAKES PLACE OUTDOORS, such as on a dock at the lake. The cabin functions as the background to this outdoor life, providing shelter on inclement days or simply extending the warm season.

AN AMERICAN ICON

The first log cabins were constructed near Wilmington, Delaware, in the early seventeenth century by Scandinavian settlers. The log cabin was claimed as a uniquely American icon when General William Henry Harrison adopted it as the symbol of his presidential campaign in 1840. Then a succession of presidents, including Polk, Buchanan, Lincoln, Johnson, and Grant, proudly traced their birthplaces to log cabins. Even President Theodore Roosevelt, born in a Manhattan brownstone, got into the act by popularizing the log cabin in which he lived while serving in the army near Medora, North Dakota. It's now preserved as a historic site.

Almost every state has famous log cabins. Some have been reconstructed, like those at Valley Forge, Pennsylvania, that sheltered General George Washington's army during the bitter winter of 1777 and those at the Log Cabin Village established by the Texas Pioneer Heritage Committee at Forest Park in Fort Worth. Many slave cabins behind Southern plantation houses have been restored. Others are individual landmarks, like the Pepin, Wisconsin, childhood home of Laura Ingalls Wilder (at left), author of the *Little House on the Prairie* books. The oldest building in Helena, Montana, is a log cabin, built around 1865.

wood frame with cable cross-bracing invisibly secures the cabin. Industrial construction techniques transform the idea of cabin from a cozy, warm blanket to an infinite view.

Cabin Pleasures Await

Cabins are reservoirs of the intangible. As different from a suburban ranch home as from a palace, a cabin is purposely a place that doesn't hold much in the tangible sense, yet holds a treasury of life's most meaningful mementos. Like a living scrapbook, cabins evoke feelings and events that no photograph could capture. A gold mine of memories is at the heart of every cabin.

What's most important? A rustic cabin represents life without pretension. A transformed cabin reminds us of the basic ecologic principle of treading gently on the earth. The traditional cabin connects us to our timeless cultural roots. And the modern cabin allows us to invent new forms through which we can expand and extend the definition of what makes a cabin.

The cabins on the following pages show how people all across the continent are building, reclaiming, or buying cabins with all this in mind. Though each cabin is unique, when all are viewed together, they reveal a compelling similarity. They show that simple can mean rich, compact can mean convenient, and informal can mean engaging.

the Rustic Cabin

RUSTIC CABINS ARE SPECIAL because of the lessons they provide and the legacy they carry of our culture. They have a timeless quality, whether they were built 300 years ago or just last summer. Their often rough-hewn character and primitive, unfinished nature give them an endearing quality. Like important historical artifacts, their presence enriches our cultural landscape.

Start with a Life-Size Model

W HEN A PROJECT LOOKS TOO BIG
TO TACKLE, it's sometimes helpful
to start with a working model. For
some, a model means balsa or Lincoln Logs, but for Deane Hillbrand it meant building an
actual cabin, one that's modest, yet fully useful as a place
to live. Aided by the purchase of some family land near
Sturgeon Lake, Minnesota, and armed with knowledge
from a log cabin–building class, Deane began erecting
the prototype. Like early American settlers, he sized his
cabin to the logs he could handle, constructing a 12-ft.
by 18-ft. place.

He started the project with some nearby dead elm
trees but soon moved on to other available timber: lighter
aspen, balsam, and birch. Scavenging for castoff windows,
flooring, and roofing materials in Minneapolis, he incorporated the found materials in the cabin. Aided with a
huge amount of sweat equity, he figures that his out-of-
pocket cost for both cabin and building education was
about $2,000.

Low-cost construction often translates into pleasing
simplicity. Here, the simple life offers an easy elegance as

**BATHED IN FILTERED SUNSHINE, THE CABIN NESTLES IN
THE FOREST.** Isolated from neighbors, the site promotes solitude, interrupted only by the sound of
the stream and a chorus of songbirds.

IN A SINGLE ROOM EVERY CORNER HAS A PURPOSE:
heat, food preparation and dishwashing, dining,
and library. A movable ladder provides access to
the sleeping loft. The open plan is easy to heat
in the winter and ventilate in the summer.

RUSTIC LIVING GETS THE JOB DONE.
The sink, which has no running
water, drains to the outside.
Deane Hillbrand brings in buck-
ets of fresh water. Heating and
cooking are provided by the
basic wood-burning stove.

well. Deane brings in his own drinking water and bathes
in the nearby stream or uses his solar hot-water shower.
Candlelight complements the electricity. Though the
cabin is only a single room, the space is defined by activities: food preparation, socializing, and reading on the main
level, with sleeping accommodations in the loft above.
From this cozy world, he can sketch and calculate as he
prepares logs and timber frames for his many new commissions. Meanwhile, down the path, across the stream,
and adjacent to the meadow, his full-scale project is finally
taking shape.

CASTOFF FURNITURE SERVES THE CABIN WELL. The table is set
with candles for a romantic evening of dining and listening
to nature's sonatas. The few windows in this cabin work
well to offer views of nature all around.

DEANE'S FULL-SCALE LOG HOME nears completion a short distance across the stream.

TINY BUT AMPLE

For a cabin that was built only as a model for a larger cabin to come, this tiny place manages to provide everything the owner needs in the meantime. Built near Sturgeon Lake, Minnesota, the cabin is basic in every way. South of the stream that divides the property, the main house is still being built.

Cabin

Forest

Path

Field

Garage

House

N

THE COMMUNITY LIBRARY is attached to the back wall. If you bring a new book to the cabin, you have to take one away.

SLEEPING IS COZY IN THE LOFT, with a window for ventilation and a light for evening reading. The loft's low-head height works for Deane, because he stores and changes his clothes on the main floor.

RUSTIC BUT SUFFICIENT

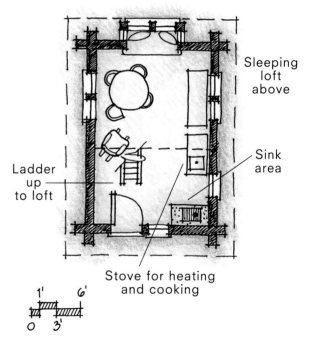

All-purpose room

Sleeping loft above

Sink area

Ladder up to loft

Stove for heating and cooking

1'   6'
0   3'

A PASSION BECOMES AN OCCUPATION

A lot of people who build their own log cabins learn the craft through one of the country's many log-building schools. The students are usually not interested in learning a trade but in learning to build something for themselves. However, some professional log-home builders got started by attending such a school and trying out their skills on a modest cabin for themselves. After friends ask for help with their own cabins, the builders find themselves with a new full-time job. That's what happened with the owner of this cabin, Deane Hillbrand, who now builds log and timberframe houses for a living.

AFTER FRIENDS ASK FOR HELP, THE BUILDERS FIND THEMSELVES WITH A NEW FULL-TIME JOB.

The Community Cabin

THE CABIN HIDES IN THE PINES AT THE BEACH. Its colors, character, and materials blend in with the natural surroundings. A soft morning light arrives at the entry and sleeping porch above.

A SERIES OF PINE ARCHWAYS, leading from the porch though the dining room to the kitchen, contribute to the cabin's circle motif. The pine logs were soaked and then bent under pressure to create the arches. The pine trestle table and benches were created by a local carpenter.

JIM AND JAN STEPHENSON BEGAN SPENDING SUMMERS at Big Sand Lake in northern Minnesota back when their children were little and beach activities were a big attraction. They often rented at Iowa Beach where other friends and professional colleagues had created a summer community. Sharing space, food, boats, and baby-sitters became a way of life. When the Chrisman cabin there was put up for sale in 1989, they snapped it up with friends Ken and Andrea Hjelm. The three-bedroom cabin with sleeping porch became their community gathering place for the summer.

The Adirondack-style cabin was built in 1938 by a local craftsman, Johnny Josephson, who created many fine summer places in the area. It features a 19-ft. by 27-ft. central living and dining hall. A stair festooned with a diamond willow rail rises to the loft and bedrooms above. The native split-fieldstone fireplace ascends to the cathedral ceiling and contains a mantel from the previous cabin on the site. The room is wrapped in a warm knotty pine. A windowed porch with a raftered ceiling parallels the lake shore to the southwest. A bedroom, bath, and kitchen

flank the rear of the structure. Sitting atop the front entry is a sleeping porch that catches morning light, a lake view, and the call of the day's beach activities.

Scale and detail are treasured in this cabin, which features many fine built-ins. A circle motif is expressed in archways from the social hall to the porch and the kitchen as well as the wagon wheel light fixture in the living room made by Jan's father. A half circle window lets light enter high in the porch, and the theme is picked up again with headboards on the beds.

When their children grew big enough, a bunk house was added over the garage, along with another bath and a sauna. Strong family ties are a common cabin theme, but in this cabin they extend to a summer community of friends.

VERTICAL AND HORIZONTAL PINE HALF LOGS are used in the hutch cabinet. Similar vertical logs create the entry door. The structural frame of log beams and purlins supports the floor decking.

AN OPEN HALF-LOG TREAD STAIRWAY IS EMBELLISHED with an idiosyncratic twig railing. This railing extends to the loft rail with an overlook to the living room.

THE SPLIT-FIELDSTONE FIREPLACE CASTS A WARM GLOW on a world of knotty pine in the living area of the cabin. This hearth room acts as a hub for all the activities of the cabin, with connections to bedrooms, bath, porches, and kitchen.

ON BIG SAND LAKE

This site is all about gathering the family at the lake, a ritual for many Americans. Families meet here every summer to swim, fish, hike, and catch up. And though parents grow old and children grow up and go away, the sense of family—like the sense of the lake—is constant.

Garage/guest cabin

Main cabin

Lake

N

A SLEEPING PORCH IS A SPECIAL FEATURE IN THIS SUMMER CABIN. The tarp can be rolled down for storm protection and off-season enclosure. Original casement windows swing in to an adjoining bedroom.

A SUMMER RETREAT

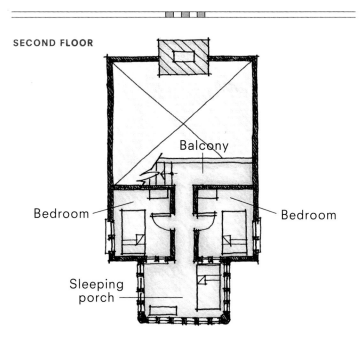

SECOND FLOOR

Balcony

Bedroom

Bedroom

Sleeping porch

FIRST FLOOR

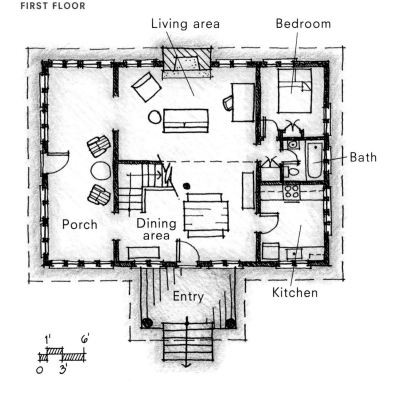

Living area

Bedroom

Bath

Porch

Dining area

Kitchen

Entry

1'　6'

0　3'

THE SHARED CABIN

Unlike houses, cabins are often shared, and that sharing happens in two ways: shared ownership within a family and shared ownership by friends. Sharing with friends makes sense. The adults enjoy each other's company and love to see their children playing together. Then there's the economic incentive—it's a lot easier to afford half a cabin than a whole one.

SHARING A CABIN WITH PEOPLE OUTSIDE OF YOUR FAMILY MAKES FOR A MEMORABLE EXPERIENCE.

Earlier, we talked about intimacy in cabins; but sharing cabins with people outside your immediate family and not worrying so much about privacy makes for a memorable experience.

Another form of sharing takes place when owners invite family or friends to come for a visit.

LOW MORNING LIGHT ENTERS THE LAKESIDE PORCH. Water activities can be enjoyed
and supervised from here, and southwest sunsets can be viewed over the lake.
The porch provides extra sleeping accommodations and fresh air.

A Family Tradition

THE SUMMER CABIN HAS A SPECIAL PLACE in the history of American cabins, when people felt the need to ward off disease by living in the fresh air—often sleeping on a porch. Carl and Barbara Solberg retain one of these historic archetypes and annually trek from Port Chester, New York, to Chetek, Wisconsin, for their dose of fresh-air living. Inherited from Barbara's family, the cabin exemplifies casual life at the lake. In the old days, the family arrived in Chetek by train and took a launch to the cabin. The boat returned twice a week to take orders for groceries and other necessities.

Built at the turn of the last century, the cabin is simple and straightforward in all respects. An inner sanctum, or hearth room, is surrounded by sleeping rooms, kitchen, and north and east porches. Originally, an outhouse, ice house, wood shed, and laundry shed flanked the cabin. Ice was cut from the lake in winter and preserved for summer use; wood was cut to warm the cabin on chilly days and to stoke the kitchen cook stove. Although running water, a bathroom, and electricity were added long ago, the place still retains an earlier charm.

THE PAINTED ARMOIRE CREATED FOR ANNA NILSDATTER IN 1902 reflects her roots from the Hardangerfjord in Norway. Its cool summer color makes it right at home in this historic porch cabin known as "Solheim," which means "Sun House" in Norwegian.

THE FIR-LINED LIVING ROOM LIFTS HIGH TO CLERESTORY WINDOWS. The tall walls are an excellent backdrop to paintings, photographs, and tapestry. The fireplace is basically a large flue attached in the corner to masonry walls. The tall interior space inhibits cross drafts and easily draws smoke out of the room. This central room also serves as the main junction connecting bedrooms and porch.

The low roofline provides ample shade in summer, creating a cool undertow to induce ventilation. Windows in the gable ends of the hearth room let in light and air.

Cabins that remain in one family for a century accumulate special lore, which gets passed along from generation to generation. The annual growth of children is marked along the door, assorted dishes are remembered for their ancestral connections, and a special book carries notes from a distant cousin. One of the Solbergs' treasured mementos is a 1902 hand-adorned armoire created for Barbara's grandmother, then known as Anna Nilsdatter.

THE LOW-SLUNG CABIN RESTS UNDER A SEA OF PINES on the western shore of Lake Chetek. Canvas awnings can be dropped to protect the porch in rainy weather and to button it up after the summer season is over.

GREEN SIDING SHEATHES THE PORCHES, demonstrating that they are, after all, outside the house. Ample space exists for both dining on the north side and sitting on the east side fronting the lake. The porch floor is painted blue, a cool, restful color for summer and for easy maintenance.

PORCH AT THE LAKE

Much of the original 100-year-old cabin compound on a lake in western Wisconsin still stands, though the ice house, wood shed, and laundry shed have since gone. What remains is a classic porch cabin on a small freshwater lake with a dock, water views, and plenty of fresh air.

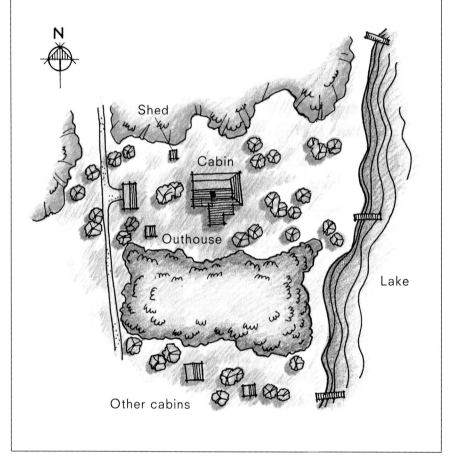

CENTRAL TO THE FAMILY

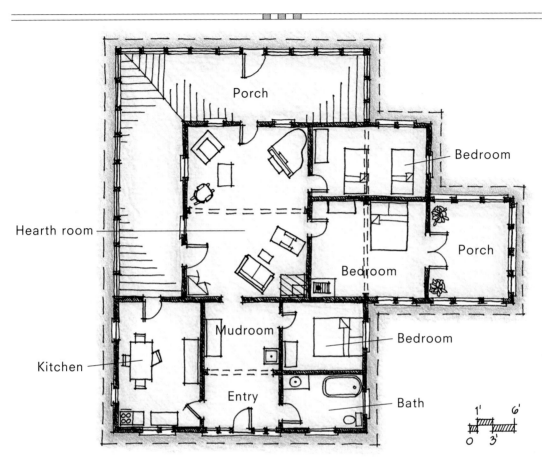

Porch

Bedroom

Hearth room

Porch

Bedroom

Mudroom

Bedroom

Kitchen

Entry

Bath

1'   6'

0   3'

THE UNFINISHED WALLS IN THE KITCHEN
provide excellent opportunities to build
shelves between the studs and create
visible storage of canisters, food para-
phernalia, and cookware. In other words,
nothing is hard to find. Double-hung windows can be opened top and bottom to
cross-ventilate this warm summer room.

IN THE ENTRY IS A COLLEC-TION OF SUMMER PLAY-THINGS, raincoats, and memorabilia. Historically, the principal entry was through the porch off the lake; this entry served as access out back to sheds beyond.

ESCAPING TO THE COUNTRY

Not so many generations ago, there was a tradition that, in the summers, the mother would take her brood out of the city—where her kids could contract tuberculosis or polio—and head to the country and the fresh air. A form of cabin was created that was predominantly a porch, although a few rooms would be insulated and could be warmed up (the main one was often called the hearth room). This cabin is in that lineage. A lot of living took place on the porch—and still does today. In the early 1900s, stoves, ice boxes, and sinks were out on the porch. The only thing that wasn't there was the source of heat.

As rampant disease became less of a threat, porches were generally converted into heatable rooms. The kitchen and bedroom parts of the porch were enclosed first. We no longer associate fresh air with protection from disease, and we now use cabins in all seasons.

A Cabin of a Different Stripe

ARK TWAIN NATIONAL FOREST lies in southeastern Missouri; and off its northeast corner, about 40 miles in from the Mississippi River, lies the 1,700-acre Coldwater Outing and Game Preserve. There, 45 cabins are clustered around a lodge adjacent to a dammed-up river and swimming basin. The cabins are nestled into the surrounding hillsides or perched along the glistening streams.

The Evans cabin was built in 1927 of oak logs for $500. The logs were squared, then blackened with creosote, and embellished with lime mortar chinking. Built into the west bank of the enclave, the Evans cabin sits atop a partial basement, which opens to an eastern view and morning light.

The cabin originally had a porch to the east, a center hearth room, a kitchen, small bedrooms, and a storage porch to the west. The eastern porch has since been converted to bedrooms, and the tiny northwestern bedroom was attached to the kitchen as an eating area. The back porch was remodeled to bring plumbing facilities indoors while still providing a rear entry. A north door provides access to outdoor living on the deck.

BECAUSE THE CABIN IS BUILT INTO A HILLSIDE, the basement door is a walk-out, opening to the east. The "Dunworkin" sign suggests the leisurely nature of the cabin and of the people who enjoy using it.

THE HEARTH ROOM IS A WONDER OF TEXTURE, from the inverted pan ceiling of lacquered bead-board pine to the darkened oak log walls with brilliantly contrasting white chinking, to the eclectic mix of stuff inside, including this zinc-top bar.

For the past 50 years, the cabin and the surrounding camp have served as a retreat for Bob and Jane Evans and their family from St. Louis. Used in all seasons, the cabin has a special connection to nature. Stories have been shared around its warm hearth by generations of family members. Its modest kitchen has yielded many memory-making dinners after a fall hunt. In summer, children have bounded out of doors to the dammed-up river. And the zebra design of this unique retreat provides an iconographic image to take back to city life.

PART OF A CABIN COMMUNITY

Roughly 40 miles from the Mississippi River, this cabin is part of a tiny valley community of 45 rustic cabins in the Coldwater Outing and Game Preserve. All owners have access to the main lodge and to a swimming hole, which was created by damming the small river. Sitting on a hillside, the Evans cabin catches eastern views and receives the morning light.

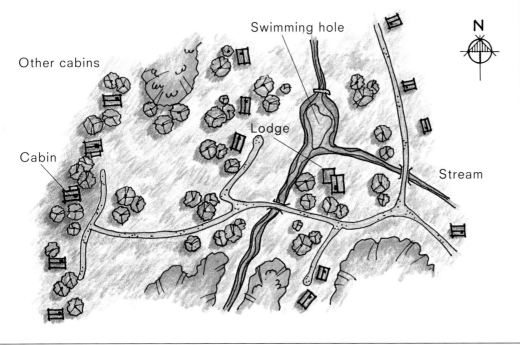

Swimming hole

Other cabins

Lodge

Cabin

Stream

N

THE EVANS CABIN, LIKE MANY IN THE GAME PRESERVE, nestles into a hillside, where its roofline presents a low profile in the forest. The cabin's black-and-white striping is a combination of creosote-treated logs and lime mortar chinking.

A CENTRAL FIREPLACE OF LOCAL SPONGE ROCK anchors the hearth room, and a skylight was added to illuminate the hearth. The 28-ft.-long room has three distinct areas: one for dining, one for sitting by the hearth, and another for reading. Plain wooden floors and ceiling contrast with the black-and-white log walls.

ONE OF THE CABIN'S ORIGINAL PORCHES was converted to a bathroom when the first owners decided to install indoor plumbing (before the current owners bought the cabin). The logs from the original porch provide a rustic setting for the old clawfoot tub.

A PLAN OF BASIC TASTES

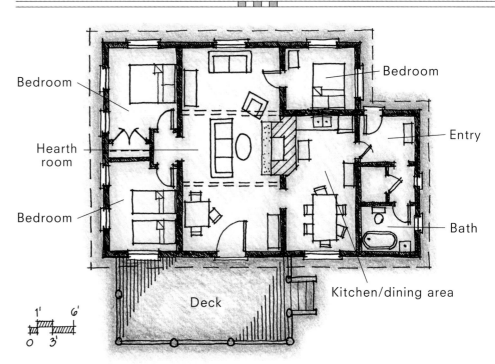

Bedroom

Hearth room

Bedroom

Bedroom

Entry

Bath

Kitchen/dining area

Deck

1'   6'
0   3'

A CABIN ROUNDUP

Most cabins are isolated structures on private land hidden away in forests or along lake shores. Others, new and old, are clustered in communities such as the Coldwater Outing and Game Preserve. They are grouped together to amortize costs or to share amenities, camaraderie, and sometimes security.

Coldwater is one of the oldest recreational associations in the Midwest. In 1924, when Missouri Fish and Game Commission chairman Frank Wielandy failed to have the land declared a state park, he organized private citizens from St. Louis and St. Genevieve to purchase the site. Up to 9,000 acres were eventually acquired, and a membership of 175 was proposed. When the federal government established the Mark Twain National Forest, 1,700 acres remained, and 45 cabins were created to share this resource. In 1926, a central lodge was built adjacent to the dammed-up Coldwater Creek, which became the swimming pond. Many other shared amenities have been added, including tennis courts, baseball diamond, trails, and trout pond.

ONE OF THE ORIGINAL BEDROOMS has windows to the south and west for good cross-ventilation.

COOKING IN THE CABIN-WIDE KITCHEN/DINING AREA is accomplished on the wood-burning stove, which vents into the chimney it shares with the hearth-room fireplace. At the far end is the dining room table, which doubles as a meeting place as well as an eating place.

Steps up a Hillside

ESTLED INTO THE SIDE OF A HILL and overlooking a lake in Solon Springs, Wisconsin, is a little yellow cottage with an even smaller yellow annex at the end of a short stepped passageway. Lore has it that the Goodrich family needed to connect two pre-existing structures so a nanny could have easy access to a newborn child. Some crafty carpenter was hired to design and build this charming connection, creating a lovely scene on the side of the hill.

The main cabin is based on a classic turn-of-the-century porch design with views over Upper St. Croix Lake. Daylight streams into a high central hearth room from above through two dormers. To reflect the light, the central room is lined with fiberboard painted white. A stone fireplace of local fieldstone backs up to the kitchen. Over time, some of the porch was filled in to create dining space and to expand the kitchen.

Originally, the family would stay only for the summer, and everyone slept, ate, and socialized on the wrap-around porch. Fresh air was considered an early preventive health measure, essential to ward off tuberculosis and polio.

THE STEPPED PASSAGEWAY TO THE BEDROOM UP THE HILL has a unique scale, with corresponding stepped roofs. The yellow clapboard forms are simply detailed and eloquently scaled, each resembling a tiny cottage. To their knowledge, the owners believe that the cottage was always painted yellow, and they respect that original decision in their careful maintenance of this cabin.

THE PORCH, WHICH OVERLOOKS UPPER ST. CROIX LAKE TO THE EAST, can now be seasonally adjusted with both screens and windows for extended use. A sunrise breakfast or spying on water activities can be enjoyed from here. The Demgens have also added a double bed for use on hot sultry nights.

CONNECTING CABIN TO NATURE

Stepped up the side of a small hill that overlooks Upper St. Croix Lake in northwestern Wisconsin, this little yellow cabin is actually a combination of two original structures. The small room to the west and the larger cabin to the east are original. The one-person-wide connection was added by previous owners.

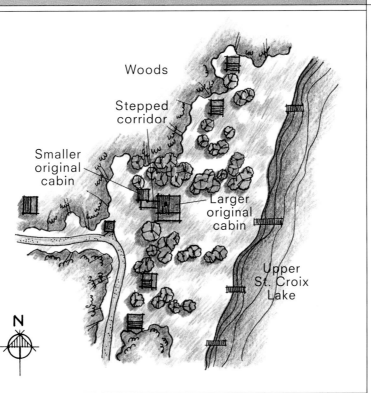

Woods

Stepped corridor

Smaller original cabin

Larger original cabin

Upper St. Croix Lake

N

Sleeping on the porch provided that needed exposure to the outside.

The Goodriches have passed the cabin along to other owners, currently Bob and Emily Demgen, but the beautiful character of its yellow stepped form has been preserved with loving care. For the Demgens, the small adjunct bedroom serves the needs of visiting grandchildren and guests or as a get-away room where one can escape from the hustle and bustle of summer cabin life.

A CHARMING SLEEPING ROOM WITH TWIN BEDS is at the end of the long, gently inclined corridor atop the hill. This space was previously a separate guest cabin but now is a connected guest bedroom. The hipped ceiling reflects the roof form.

AN AMATEUR EFFORT FEW ARCHITECTS COULD MATCH

What's special about this cabin is the link that joins the larger original porch cabin and the smaller guest cabin and the way it was scaled to make the whole composition feel like a hillside cascade of tiny cottages. In reality, it's simply a stepped corridor, but its image and presence are greater than that.

From the outside, the corridor presents an intimately scaled structure, in which each section looks no larger

than a space for one. This is what lifts the cabin above the normal and into the realm of the special. Though obviously an amateur effort, few architects could have pulled off this intimate connection as well.

CABIN EVOLUTION

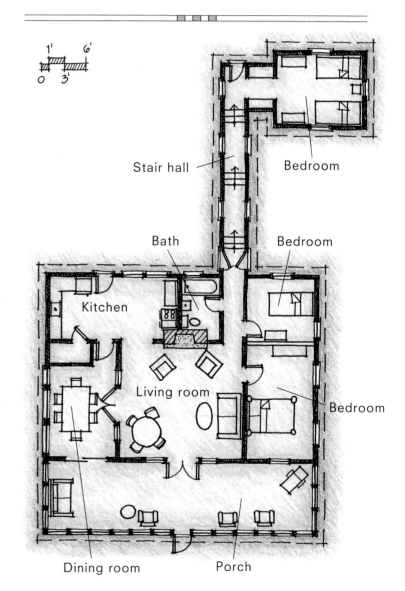

Stair hall

Bedroom

Bath

Bedroom

Kitchen

Living room

Bedroom

Dining room

Porch

THE MAIN LIVING SPACE HAS A HIGH CEILING, providing both light and ventilation. The ceiling is sheathed in painted fiberboard, which reflects the dormer light. Local fieldstone was used to make the fireplace.

Big at Heart

CELEBRATING A 40TH BIRTHDAY has been known to trigger a midlife crisis, leading to divorce, depression, or despair. Instead of those more extreme choices, Lois Schwob opted to attend log-building school. In a radical departure from urban motherhood in 1972, Lois joined the Ron Brantigan Log School in Hinckley, Minnesota, to learn how to wield a chainsaw and hoist a purlin. After 10 days at the school, a seed was planted, though it took another decade for it to bear fruit.

Over the next five years, Lois and her husband, John, searched for land, finally selecting a lot high above Lake Superior. It took another five years to purchase logs. By 1981, Lois returned to the Brantigan School, this time with John, to buy the school's latest log cabin construction project. Finally, over the course of 1982, with the help of family and friends, they assembled, roofed, and personalized this modest structure, adding a sauna, solar shower, and outhouse, turning their rustic cabin into a real getaway.

WHERE IT SITS ON A SMALL HILL, the little log cabin blends into the landscape of trees and grass. The log form even suggests the stack of firewood that sits out back.

THE COVERED PORCH IS AN IMPORTANT EXTENSION OF THIS TINY CABIN. It promotes outdoor living even on a rainy day, provides storage for cross-country skis in winter, and offers relief from the sun on a warm summer day. It's a great place to hang out with guests and neighbors or just to sit and enjoy the countryside.

A SHIP'S LADDER PROVIDES ACCESS TO THE LOFT over the main living area. When not in use, the ladder is stored in the loft to free up needed living space. The loft stays warm as heat rises on winter nights, but with a window open on summer nights the breeze flows upward, providing cool ventilation.

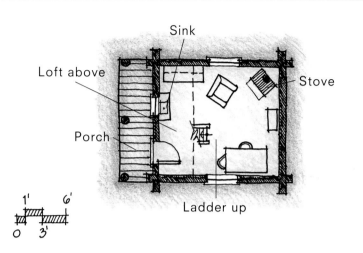

Sink

Loft above

Stove

Porch

Ladder up

1' 6'

0 3'

ONE ROOM AS A WHOLE HOME

It takes some imagination to take an open 14-ft. by 16-ft. room and jigger its simple rectangular plan into a working home—if only for weekends and vacations. But that's the type of planning that has to take place if a family is going to use the room for a variety of different needs: from sleeping to cooking, from reading to entertaining.

For some, a 14-ft. by 16-ft. room is small, even for a master bedroom; but for Lois and John Schwob, this tiny, changing space is everything. After sunup, it's the communal hub around which the household revolves, and the table often seats 10 for a candlelit dinner. At night it's a bedroom for four to six sleepers, as long as privacy is not an issue. Each corner of the cabin has a unique purpose: cooking, heating, library, or projects. Despite its modest size, the room seems much bigger, thanks to the loft and porch, which let the Schwobs move up or out. From the porch, the family can watch the sun rise over the lake with that first cup of coffee or enjoy the moon's reflection with a final brandy.

DESPITE ITS MODEST SIZE, THE ROOM SEEMS MUCH BIGGER, THANKS TO THE LOFT AND PORCH.

There is more to consider when siting a cabin than finding the best view. There is its orientation to the sun, which was done well here. The cabin is skewed 30° off the north–south axis to take full advantage of the sun—especially important in this northern climate.

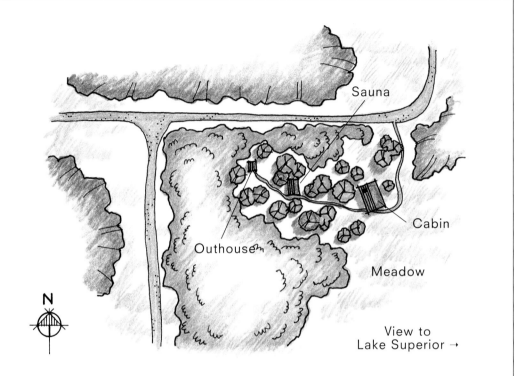

Sauna

Cabin

Outhouse

Meadow

N

View to
Lake Superior →

BECAUSE THE CABIN DOESN'T HAVE RUNNING WATER, the owners limit the amount they have to import by collecting rainwater. Warmed by a solar heater, the soft rainwater makes for luxurious showers.

FANCY HARDWARE ISN'T NECESSARY for making great meals in this kitchen, which is an alcove in the main room. Many hearty meals for 10 have been whipped up in this small space.

WHAT IS IT ABOUT CABIN LIVING that inspires crafts? Relatives feel free to leave mementos, fashioned from local materials, in appreciation for a weekend visit. Relaxation leads to whittling, sketching, bird watching, or gathering wildflowers.

Maintaining Integrity

THE SINGLE-STORY CABIN, SURROUNDED BY FLOWERING PLANTS AND SHRUBS, sits on a comparatively large plot of land. "One of the things I like about the cottage is that it's on a grand piece of property," says Shannon McLean. In keeping with the custom of painting only the window trim and doors of beach homes, Shannon picked a bright blue for the trim.

THE OWNER DECIDED TO KEEP AS MUCH OF THE ORIGINAL cabin's personality as possible, including the Dutch door main entry. The only major change she made in the interior was converting a tiny bedroom into a bath, where she installed an old clawfoot bathtub.

FASHION DESIGNER SHANNON MCLEAN BELIEVES luck led her to a tiny cabin nestled amid huge, multimillion-dollar homes in Wainscott, a posh Hamptons resort area on New York's Long Island. She was looking for her car on a dirt road behind the beach when she spied the cabin and a homemade for-sale sign on the lawn. To her, the place "represents exactly what the Hamptons were meant to be," so, sight unseen, she told the owner she wanted to buy it. Ten days later she moved in.

Shannon learned that the cabin was one of several built in 1932 so members of a large family could each have their own vacation home. Originally, it was on the beach but was moved to its present site after a big hurricane in the late 1930s (the other cabins next door are behind a large hedge). The outside, including the roof, was built of cedar, which has weathered nicely over time. Though the inside was a "shambles" when Shannon bought it, the structure was sound. "It never rotted because the cedar wood is so oily," notes Shannon.

"It was important for me to keep the integrity of what the cabin was for—a place to walk in with sandy feet and

THE KITCHEN IS HIDDEN BEHIND AN OPEN BAR opposite the fireplace, with a dining table and chairs conveniently positioned nearby. Though the cabin didn't have indoor running water when it was built, that was added before Shannon bought it.

plop down," she says. "It already had a soul so I just wanted to doll it up a bit." So she invested in a spray gun, mask, and paper suit and sprayed the interior white from floor to ceiling. Then she furnished it with things she found at tag sales and thrift shops, establishing a floral theme to match the cornflower blue trim on the exterior.

When the days grow shorter and colder, Shannon knows it's time to close the cabin for another year. So she brushes the sand out the door, throws sheets over the furniture, and says good-bye until the next summer.

THE BRICK FIREPLACE IS THE FOCUS OF THE GREAT ROOM, which has an area for sitting and two areas for eating. The bare floors are easy to keep clean, since Shannon just sweeps the sand she tracks in back out the door. She purposefully didn't cover the walls perfectly when she spray–painted them, letting slivers of the original wood show through here and there.

PART OF A SEASIDE COMMUNITY

Once part of a small group of vacation cabins built for a large family, this little cabin still sits suburb-style amid a community of homes overlooking the Atlantic Ocean. Though it's not on the beach, it's near enough to catch the views, sounds, and smells of the ocean.

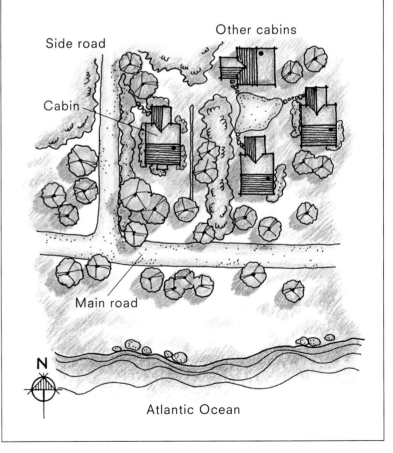

Side road
Other cabins
Cabin
Main road
N
Atlantic Ocean

SIMPLE SHELTER

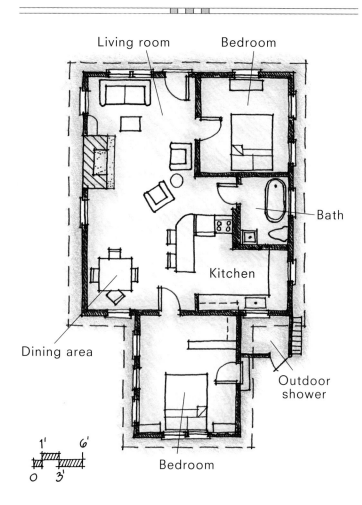

Living room

Bedroom

Bath

Kitchen

Dining area

Outdoor shower

Bedroom

1' 6'

0 3'

SHANNON'S BEDROOM HAS JUST ENOUGH SPACE to walk around a double bed. "I go to sleep listening to the ocean. There's nothing better than that quiet sound," says Shannon. The door to the left leads to an outoor shower where she rinses off after returning from the beach.

THESE BUILT-IN SHELVES were part of the original cabin.

FINDING POTENTIAL IN THE ORDINARY

Sometimes the ordinary can be extraordinary, as in this simple cabin on New York's Long Island. The owner, Shannon McLean, found a basic box and made it special. Part of what makes it special is that she spray-painted the whole thing white—walls, floors, ceiling, doors. Outside, it's a wood-sided cube and a bit dark; inside, it's light and cheery. With the ever-present white as a background, the cabin is decorated with colorful elements to give it life.

HAVING THE EYE TO SEE THROUGH TO THE POTENTIAL IS A RARE SKILL.

Older cabins like this simply didn't have a lot of windows, so they're naturally rather dark. But Shannon wanted more brightness, and the white was a simple, straightforward solution.

Having the eye to see through to the potential of a building and then clarify its essential qualities are rare skills. Shannon didn't try to do much with the cabin, but what she did do brought out its best.

Rustic Oasis

THE REIS FAMILY was among the select group of St. Louis families who, beginning in the 1920s, headed for the cool retreat of the forest at the beginning of summer and stayed there until the city cooled off. They took the train along the Mississippi River as far south as St. Genevieve where they were met by a fleet of Model-Ts, which transported them to the forest some 40 miles away. There the Reises took up summer residence in their new cabin at Coldwater Outing and Game Preserve, where they escaped the heat by floating on the river. In the fall, they returned to participate in the annual hunt.

The cabin is set on the western slope of a valley with a river, community swimming pond, and central lodge below. Anchored on the hillside with a sturdy poured concrete foundation, it was intended to last for generations. The cabin was built of pine logs hewn from the site, but finer finishes were added of oak plank floors and cypress board ceilings. Because Mr. Reis ran a lumberyard specializing in millwork for churches, colleges, and other public buildings, he thought it fitting to add decorative arched doorways to this otherwise rustic oasis.

THE CABIN IS BANKED INTO AN EAST-FACING HILL so that warm southern sun filters onto the deck. Life's daily cycle starts with the sunrise and ends when the sun sinks behind the western hills.

THE LIVING ROOM FEATURES A LARGE FIREPLACE of local sponge rock with a hewn pine mantel. The room is large enough to accommodate a sitting area, game table, and writing desk.

THE LARGEST OF THE TWO PORCHES ON THE CABIN
lets out onto the east-facing deck, where the log
railing echoes the construction of the whole.

In the 1960s, the cabin was passed along to the
Niederlander family, one of whose early guests was Jim
Bowen. Jim remembers well his first visit—he dined on
fried squirrel. Then, 20 years later, he had the opportunity
to purchase the property from the Niederlanders, and he
and his family have enjoyed it ever since.

While other families take their greatest enjoyment
from summer sojourns or the fall hunt, Jim's special season
is winter. Nestled with family and friends around a roaring fire under a full moon or a soft snowfall creates special
moments found only in cabins.

A TIGHT-KNIT CABIN COMMUNITY

A series of small streams
course through the wrin-
kles of the hilly Coldwater
Outing and Game Pre-
serve. A dam on the
largest stream backs up
enough water to maintain
a cool swimming hole,
where all can take refuge
from the summer heat.
Most of the 45 cabins in
this community were built
in the 1920s and 1930s.

Swimming hole

Other
cabins

Cabin

Lodge

Automobile
access

N

Stream

FINDING COOL SHADE

This cabin is about shade and summertime. It's built into a hill, and one porch opens downhill and looks toward the surrounding cabin community and the dammed-up stream that serves as the local swimming hole. Though there's abundant shade here, thanks to the heavy forest, this porch captures the low morning light. And in the heat of the afternoon, it stays cool, because the hillside protects it from the western sun.

IN THE HEAT OF THE AFTERNOON, THE HILLSIDE PROTECTS THE CABIN FROM THE WESTERN SUN.

In the summer, the owners come here to escape the heat of St. Louis and cool off under the dense canopy of trees and in the refreshing currents of air moving off the water. Cooler air drops downhill and passes through the cabin, maintaining a nice air flow.

There's also a sunny breakfast porch at the southwest corner of the cabin. Because it catches the cool down-flowing air, this porch is great for outdoor cooking. Here the owners can enjoy nature—without the mosquitoes.

THANKS TO AMPLE PORCHES AND LOTS OF WINDOWS, the outside is never far away. On cool nights, the owners close the frosted windows onto the porch and light a fire in the fireplace.

AN INTIMATE KITCHEN FEATURES THE BASICS, including built-in storage and the original cast-iron sink, which is big enough to make dishwashing a shared task.

THE PINE LOGS STILL DISPLAY THEIR ORIGINAL CHINKING, untouched since 1928, and the cypress ceiling casts a warm glow in the living room. Decorative white door frames are the originals and reflect the first owner's interest in church millwork. Morning light from the eastern porch enters the living room, and north and south windows provide airflow across the space.

HEARTH AT THE CENTER

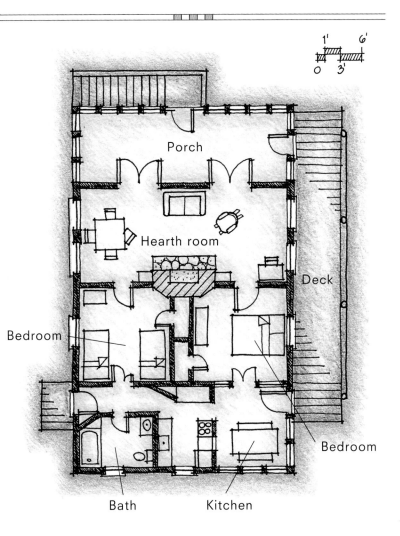

A Chain of Perfect Cabins

THE GUEST QUARTERS ABOVE THE STORAGE GARAGE offers a view of the vast expanse of Lake Superior. This loftlike building is similar to storage sheds found on rustic Scandinavian farms.

ALTHOUGH ARCHITECT EDWIN LUNDIE HAD NEVER been to Scandinavia, his design of these small timberframe cabins reflects a deep understanding of the traditional form found in Norway and Sweden.

IN POST–WORLD WAR II CHICAGO, a Dr. Curtis sought respite from summer heat in the cool, forested shoreline of Lake Superior. To get just the retreat he wanted, Curtis commissioned St. Paul architect Edwin Lundie to design a cabin for him. Lundie was known for modeling his cabins after rustic village structures found in hamlets in Norway and Sweden.

For the Curtis family, Lundie created four timberframe structures along a thin plane of shoreline above a rocky ledge. The first building encountered, where the entry road intersects the ledge, is a garage with guest quarters that were conceived as a loft. A tiny stairway rises to a single room above the precarious cliffs. Where the ledge slopes gently downward toward the shore, Lundie constructed a guest cabin with paired bunk beds built next to an oversize fireplace. A modest kitchenette and bathroom were added to create a self-sufficient structure, one that could be considered an outpost to the main cabin. Proceeding down the ledge, there is a timberframe woodshed and then the two-bedroom main cabin.

The main cabin features a combination living room/dining room with windows looking out across the vast

The road to this trio of timberframe cabins runs perpendicular to the shore of Lake Superior and then parallel to it, along a thin strip of rocky beach. Perhaps it was the Scandinavian texture of water, rock, and sky that inspired architect Edwin Lundie to compose this suite of cabins in the style of nineteenth-century homes built in Norway and Sweden.

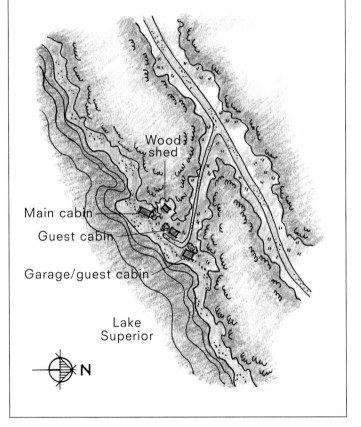

expanse of Lake Superior. At a 90° angle is a shorter glass wall that opens to a view of the shoreline. The room features another great stone fireplace made from local granite, which is visibly framed by a timber truss, purlins, and rafters of local white pine. Elaborate carving on the truss highlights its mortise-and-tenon joinery. The exterior is composed of panels of diagonal siding between timberframe posts. The whole is painted a Scandinavian red.

THE CORNER COLUMNS OF THE FOUR STRUCTURES ARE SIMILAR, yet each is unique. They join together the main structural elements of the cabins. Edwin Lundie's cabins were said by local carpenters to fit together like finely crafted furniture.

THE HEARTH ROOM IN THE MAIN CABIN doubles as living room and dining room, providing spectacular views of the lake. The fireplace is made from local granite, and the truss, purlins, and rafters are local white pine.

THE ARCHITECT DESIGNED SEVERAL
PIECES OF FURNITURE FOR THESE
CABINS, such as a chest in the
guest loft and this kitchenette
cabinet in the guest cabin. Pine
doors close the kitchenette off
when not in use. Lundie also
designed lighting fixtures and
door and drawer hardware for
many of his cabins.

AN ENSEMBLE OF CABINS

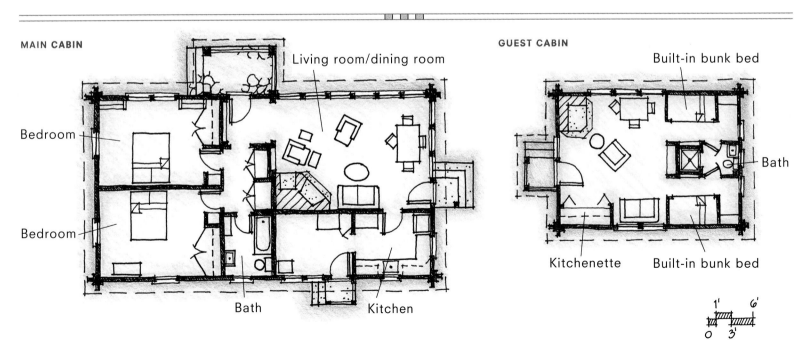

MAIN CABIN

Living room/dining room

Bedroom

Bedroom

Bath

Kitchen

GUEST CABIN

Built-in bunk bed

Bath

Kitchenette

Built-in bunk bed

1'   6'

0   3'

BUILDINGS LIKE FURNITURE

Edwin Lundie was a designer of fine homes for clients in and around St. Paul, Minnesota, from 1922 to 1971. For a few of those clients, he designed cabins on or near Lake Superior. Although his urban home designs drew from European and New England themes, such as French country and Cape Cod, his cabin designs were drawn from Scandinavian influences.

Perhaps his accessibility to excellent Finnish, Norwegian, and Swedish craftsmen was the impetus for this new influence. He had a proclivity for designing small, finely crafted buildings; and even many of his larger homes were designed like small structures assembled together. His cabins were carefully planned and constructed, like fine pieces of furniture. They were embellished with hand-crafted light fixtures, door latches, and built-ins, each created by following a full-scale template drawing made by Lundie.

His own cabin, similar to the Curtis guest cabin, was 18 ft. by 28 ft. and included a pair of bunk beds, a massive granite fireplace, and a kitchen. It is beautifully crafted of white pine, including the corner columns, which were turned on a lathe. Other cabins contained elaborate structural timberframes finely joined by mortises and tenons.

the Transformed Cabin

ENVISIONING OPPORTUNITY WHEN FINDING a rundown shack or abandoned garage requires imagination, followed by ingenuity and effort. Structures can be dismantled, moved, and rebuilt or transformed in modest or radical ways. The inestimable value of the transformed cabin is that it offers a vital ingredient of cabin life—instantaneous lore.

Tobacco Barn to Log Cabin

STEPPING INTO LINDA AND BERNARD FLIPPIN'S CABIN is like stepping into the past. You'd swear the tiny dwelling in Virginia's Blue Ridge Mountains was built centuries ago. The truth is, the cabin wasn't constructed until 1993. What gives the cabin its authentic air is what it was made from: logs salvaged from a North Carolina tobacco barn built in the late 1800s.

Bernard was inspired to build the cabin after his neighbor Alvin Easter learned that the barn was about to be demolished. Rather than let that happen, the two men decided to rescue the beautiful hand-hewn logs and reuse them to build two log cabins. Planning ahead, they carefully numbered each of the logs as they dismantled the barn. Though that took only a long day and lots of elbow grease, they spent the next seven months, working every evening from July to November, building the 18-ft. by 19-ft. cabin.

Overlooking a valley and a little rushing creek, the cabin sits on a rock foundation, with porches front and back and a tin roof, specifically designed to enhance the sound of raindrops. To make sure the logs fit snugly,

A NEIGHBOR USED HIGHLY PRIZED WORMY CHESTNUT to build the corner cabinet, which displays family china. Linda Flippin decorated the cabin with family heirlooms, such as the photo of Bernard's great-grandfather and the rug made by her grandmother.

NESTLED IN A HOLLOW IN THE BLUE RIDGE MOUNTAINS just 200 ft. behind Bernard and Linda's brick ranch home, this tiny cabin speaks of a distant past. In addition to the logs salvaged from an old North Carolina barn, more old lumber, mostly wormy chestnut and oak, was used throughout the house as paneling, steps, and cupboards.

FURNISHED WITH ROCKING CHAIRS, the cabin's front porch provides a refuge for quiet moments. An old-fashioned white iron bed beckons invitingly through the open door, which is made of chestnut and pine planks purposefully aged to give them character.

Bernard filled the gaps between them with concrete. Though the cabin is wired for electricity, the Flippins don't use it much. They prefer to light it with candles and kerosene lamps. "We love to imagine what it was like back in the old days," says Linda. "That's why I've decorated with antiques and mementos."

The Flippins use the cabin often—especially when they want to step back in time for a change of pace. In addition to being a popular place for cookouts and sing-alongs with friends and neighbors, it's also been used for wedding and baby showers. "My little three-year-old granddaughter, Cassidy, thinks this is her playhouse," Linda says.

OLD CURIOS ADORN SHELVES built into one corner over Bernard's mother's treadle sewing machine. "We don't want to make this a showcase for anything new," says Linda. "It's the preservation of the past that interests us," she adds.

LIFE THE WAY IT WAS

It doesn't take a great deal of imagination to picture this little creek valley 150 or 200 years ago, with the same little cabin sitting right where it is today. Maintaining tradition was a distinct force in the creation of this cabin, both in preserving the old wood timbers and logs and in preserving the sense of life that was rural Virginia.

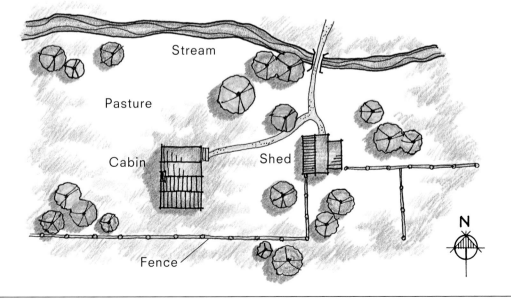

Stream

Pasture

Cabin

Shed

Fence

N

BARN REINCARNATION

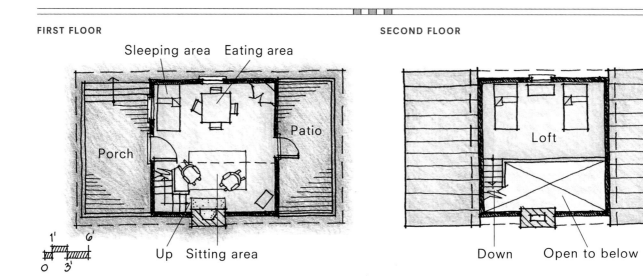

FIRST FLOOR

Sleeping area   Eating area

Porch

Patio

1'   6'

0   3'

Up   Sitting area

SECOND FLOOR

Loft

Down   Open to below

THE ESSENCE OF RECYCLING

Old log homes and timberframes have a unique ability to be recycled. Their basic nature, the way they were assembled, suggests that the elements can be fairly easily disassembled and then reassembled. It also suggests that wood can have an incredibly long lifespan.

But more than wood can be reused. Of course, the logs and timbers are the primary recyclable parts. However, the stone foundation can be recycled into fireplaces; the old cabinets turned into new cabinets; and the flooring, doors, and windows used anew.

The very memory of an old building can also be recycled. For instance, a physician fondly remembered an old cabin once owned by his parents. The doctor hired an architect to carefully re-create his family's cabin and revive his childhood memories.

THE DESIGN OF THE SLEEPING LOFT WAS KEPT SIMPLE and furnished authentically with iron beds tucked under the eaves. The floor in the loft is made of salvaged oak and chestnut boards. The only nod to modern comfort is in the insulation batts tucked between the log rafters.

A Clever Conversion

TWO COUPLES INVESTED in a vacation home on Cape Cod in the early 1980s, but decided to rent out the main house during the summer season and convert an abandoned 400-sq.-ft. garage into a small cottage where they would stay. But then they discovered that Cape Cod National Seashore regulations prohibited them from having a second home on the property. They found an ingenious way to skirt the rules: The cabin would be considered a guesthouse if it didn't contain a stove.

The couples hired Chad Floyd of Centerbrook Architects to do the renovation on a strict budget of $20,000, including architectural fees. Finding the garage structurally sound but "tired," Floyd replaced finishes inside and out, adding pine beadboard in the main living spaces and gypsum wallboard in the bedroom and bath. Then he divided the space into a living area, kitchen-eating area, bedroom, and bath, building a loft in the rafters over the kitchen for additional sleeping and storage.

Floyd was able to work within the budget by retaining many original garage features. For instance, the wooden panels in the overhead door were replaced with glass,

ARCHITECT CHAD FLOYD RETAINED THE MAIN FEATURE of the original garage—the overhead door—but altered it by inserting glass panes for the wood panels. This turned the door into a large rolling window, which makes the interior seem more open and airy. Adding the deck increased the cabin's living space by 50 percent.

A BUILT-IN LADDER MAKES THE WIDOW'S WALK EASILY ACCESSIBLE from the deck. Both outdoor rooms help increase the cabin's tiny living space, which can be used comfortably by six people at a time.

which allows light and ocean views. A roll-up screen was installed so the door could be opened during warm summer days.

Building outdoor rooms helped expand the living space. Floyd took advantage of a natural outdoor room created by a pine grove and designed a 200-sq.-ft. redwood deck within it, which conveniently fronts the door. Cooking takes place there on an outdoor grill. Building a 100-sq.-ft. redwood widow's walk on top of the garage provided a typical New England way to enjoy the impressive ocean view.

Now that the families' children have graduated from college, the adults have reclaimed the main house, and the cabin is used, in accordance with its registration, as a guesthouse by children and grandkids.

LESSONS OF THE ADAPTED GARAGE

Thanks to a large redwood deck off the rear of the cabin and a widow's walk on the roof, the roughly 21-ft. by 19-ft. former garage works for its owners like a much larger cabin. Those outdoor spaces, and the fact that cooking is done outdoors, broaden the useful area of the cabin itself.

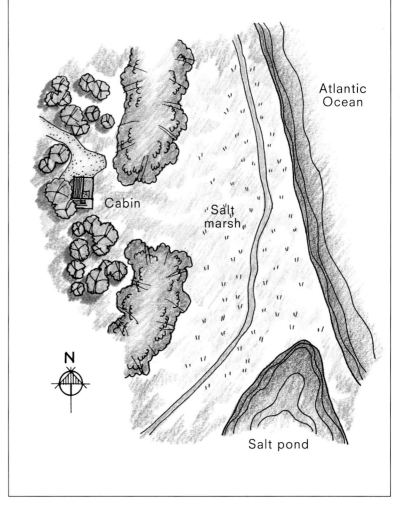

PINE BEADBOARD, TYPICAL OF CAPE COD CABINS, casts a warm glow over the interior, which is divided into areas for sitting, eating, and sleeping. The cabin was designed to sleep six. A ladder built into the wall provides easy access to the loft.

THE WIDOW'S WALK SURVEYS A DRAMATIC PANORAMA of the Atlantic Ocean set against salt marshes and ponds in the foreground and an old Coast Guard station in the background.

KEEP THE DOORS WIDE OPEN

There is a common scenario in which people hold parties in their garage. They throw open the doors and the party can overflow into the parking area or stay inside, out of the rain, if need be. This cabin on Cape Cod captures that quality, where people can be inside and outside at the same time—and all the time be part of the same summery experience.

This former garage is not immediately on the water, but it opens up to the sea air. And the widow's walk atop the cabin provides an opportunity for viewing the water and catching the breeze. The garage door opens to the east-northeast, where the early sun is cool. By the time the day warms up, the big door is in the shade.

THIS CABIN CAPTURES THAT QUALITY, WHERE PEOPLE CAN BE INSIDE AND OUTSIDE AT THE SAME TIME.

MAKING SMALL WORK LIKE BIG

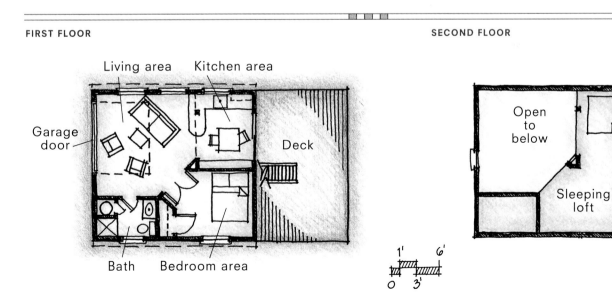

FIRST FLOOR

Living area
Kitchen area
Garage door
Deck
Bath
Bedroom area

SECOND FLOOR

Open to below
Sleeping loft

1' 6'
0 3'

Reviving a Ghost Town

IN THE EARLY 1880S WHEN GOLD WAS DIS-COVERED in the Judith Mountains, the town of Maiden, Montana, was one of the largest settle-ments in the state, with upward of 2,000 residents. But when the gold played out by the turn of the century, the town rapidly declined, leaving only a handful of min-ers, like Patrick Hanley's maternal grandfather, George Wieglenda, who settled there in 1895.

Over the course of George's life, he accumulated a homestead and other property. By 1957, when Pat in-herited some of the property, Maiden had become a his-toric ghost town, with many buildings either burned or in various stages of disintegration. After Pat restored his grandfather's log homestead as a vacation home in 1985, he decided to rescue the one-room log cabin that had once belonged to Tom Kerr, the town's saloon keeper.

In 1999, he hired contractor Bud Barta to reassemble the hand-hewn structure on a new concrete foundation about 20 ft. from its original location. The top and bottom logs had to be replaced; and because the space between the logs varied from nothing to 4 in., adequate chinking had to be added between the old logs. Pat wanted to add

THE TOM KERR CABIN IS LOCATED ACROSS A SMALL STREAM and a couple of hundred feet west of Patrick Hanley's restored vacation cabin (right background), which was his grandfather's original homestead. For 70 years, the cabin was used only for storage. In the foreground is what remains of Tom Kerr's Bouillon Saloon.

THE TOM KERR CABIN IS PROBABLY one of the original 1880 structures in Maiden, Montana. Pat had it completely modernized in 1999 after the 18-ft. by 25-ft. log cabin was moved to a new concrete foundation. One major change is the covered porch, which is wider on the eastern side than on the southern side.

THANKS TO HIS MOTHER AND SOME LOCAL SOURCES, Pat has a huge stash of old photographs showing Maiden during its heyday as a bustling mining town. His grandfather (top) stands proudly with two of his children beside one of the town's original log structures.

A CABIN WHERE ONCE A TOWN STOOD

A small creek runs through the little valley, and the Judith Mountains tower beyond. Once the site of a prospering Gold Rush town of nearly 2,000 people, all that's left of Maiden (near the town of Lewiston) is a few buildings, including this cabin and an old saloon.

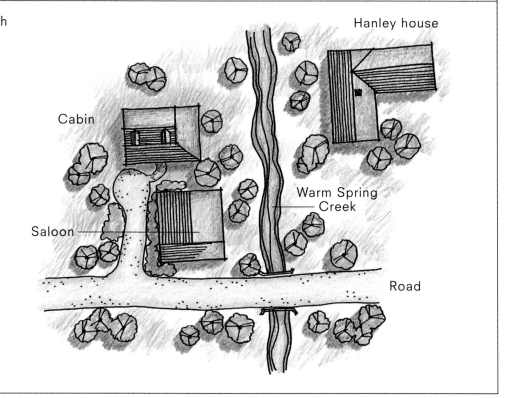

porches on the eastern and southern sides to create covered entrances, so Bud extended the roof on the eastern front and put a shed roof on the south, covering the whole with galvanized corrugated roofing that he salvaged from the original cabin and from another abandoned building. At Pat's request, Bud added two large dormers that flood the cabin with natural light.

Because Pat wanted to preserve as much of the old character of the building as he could, Bud used traditional beaded paneling on the ceiling and replaced the floor with traditional fir flooring. The doors are made of recycled rafters and beaded paneling. Most of the furnishings were things Pat found stored in the rundown cabin, along with the original bar from Tom Kerr's saloon. "My long-term plan is to decorate the cabin with antique mining, moonshining, and other original artifacts that I found in the building," Pat says.

"I'M TRYING TO BE SELECTIVE about what I put in the Tom Kerr cabin," says Pat, who found most of the furnishings in the dilapidated cabin and had them restored. Pat wants to re-create the feeling of the original cabin as much as possible.

RETAINING THE LORE

What was once a thriving Montana mining community has been reduced, or refined, to a one-room cabin repository of town memories. Tom Kerr was the town saloon keeper. In the rough frontier town of Maiden, Montana, he would've been one of the most important people around. Patrick Hanley, whose grandfather was a miner in the town, now owns much of what's left of Maiden, along with Tom Kerr's cabin. In it is a copper still and the old bar.

Whereas some cabins are recycled from pieces of other places, this cabin recycles the lore of Tom Kerr's life and times.

THIS CABIN RECYCLES THE LORE OF TOM KERR'S LIFE AND TIMES.

SUNLIGHT FROM THE DORMER WINDOWS FILLS THE INTERIOR with southern light and reflects off the fir flooring. The new propane stove is a necessary source of heat during most of the year, except in July and August. The saloon's original copper still is against the back wall, tucked under the loft.

A REMINDER OF THE PAST

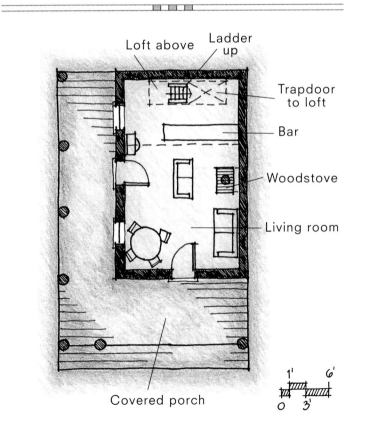

Loft above
Ladder up
Trapdoor to loft
Bar
Woodstove
Living room
Covered porch

A 12-FT.-WIDE SLEEPING LOFT WAS BUILT IN THE RAFTERS over the western end of the interior so that the cabin could be used as a guest house. The only permanent fixture in the interior is the 12-ft.-long wooden bar that came from Tom Kerr's saloon. Pat assumes his grandfather moved the bar from the saloon to the cabin when he started to use the saloon as his mining office.

An Odd Couple

David Diao, a world-class artist who teaches at the Whitney Museum of American Art in New York City, which was designed by Hungarian-born architect Marcel Breuer, has long been an avid fan of modernism and Breuer's work. When he was offered a chance to buy a Breuer-designed cabin a few years ago, he leapt at the opportunity.

"Once I saw the place I had to have it, even though it was in horrible repair," says David. The cabin is in rural Pleasant Valley about 90 miles north of New York City. "The roofs were leaking, the cypress siding was rotting, and I wasn't crazy about the attached Spartan trailer either, but how often does one get to own a Breuer?"

David discovered the origins of the odd couple: In 1949 artist Sidney Wolfson commissioned Breuer to marry his now-classic 1930s, elegantly streamlined, functionally formed, highly polished aluminum Spartan trailer with a Breuer-designed, angular, cantilevered box atop a laid-stone perch. Before David and his partner, Maureen Connor, who designs interactive video displays and teaches art at Queens College, could enjoy weekends and summers

THE SPARTAN "ROYAL MANSION" TRAILER, first produced in 1934 based on principles of aircraft technology, has been called the "Rolls Royce of trailers."

CABINS ARE ALLOWED TO BE ECCENTRIC. Like David Diao and Maureen Connor's two-in-one retreat: an open-plan residence—designed by Marcel Breuer—attached to a sleek Spartan trailer, both are greatly revered by architectural buffs. David is researching the best way to polish the trailer's aluminum shell.

MOBILE MELDS WITH STATIONARY

As unusual as it would seem, a gleaming, vintage aluminum travel trailer attached to a modernist cabin in rural Upstate New York really makes a great getaway. Just 90 miles from New York City, the odd mix of the stationary and the mobile seems to fit naturally into the woodsy landscape.

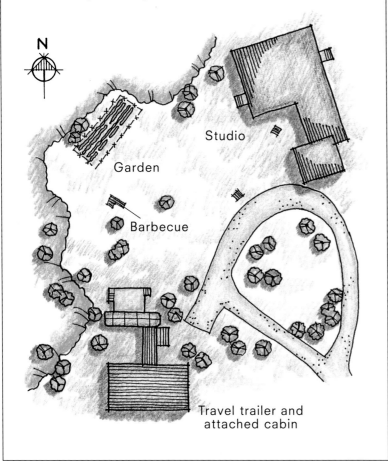

A SCREENED PORCH IS ATTACHED TO THE TRAILER. "The porch reaches out into the landscape," says David, thereby expanding the cabin's living space during summer months.

there, they had to do extensive renovations. The major things were installing a new rubber membrane roof, replacing the cypress tongue-in-groove siding, and installing a new gas stove and refrigerator in the trailer.

"I keep thinking I want to remove the trailer and put a new kitchen/living/great room wing in its place," says David, who also teaches art at Cornell University. "But as time has passed, I feel less inclined to destroy the original design. If I were to build the new wing, it would essentially make obsolete the whole function of the present living/dining/bedroom, double-fireplace space, which is the heart of Breuer's design. The latest thought is to somehow fit a good modern kitchen in the trailer. I'm still trying to think it through."

DAVID CALLS THE DOUBLE-SIDED FIREPLACE IN THE GREAT ROOM, artfully assembled from local field-stone, "the heart of Breuer's design." David and Maureen keep it blazing during the winter months as much for emotional as for practical reasons.

THE ORIGINAL OWNER USED THE TRAILER primarily as a kitchen. David, who often eats breakfast in the trailer, plans to restore the curved wood panels.

THE END OF THE TRAIL

FIRST FLOOR

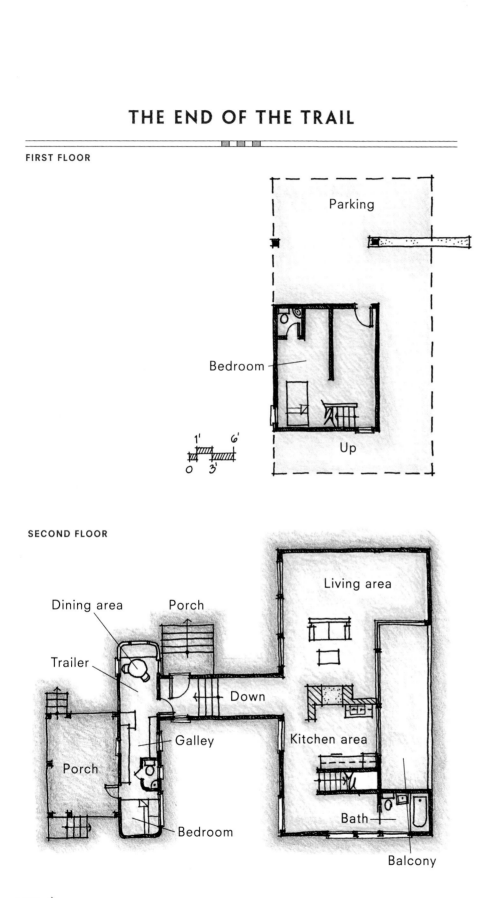

Parking

Bedroom

Up

1' 6'

0 3'

SECOND FLOOR

Dining area

Porch

Trailer

Living area

Down

Galley

Kitchen area

Porch

Bedroom

Bath

Balcony

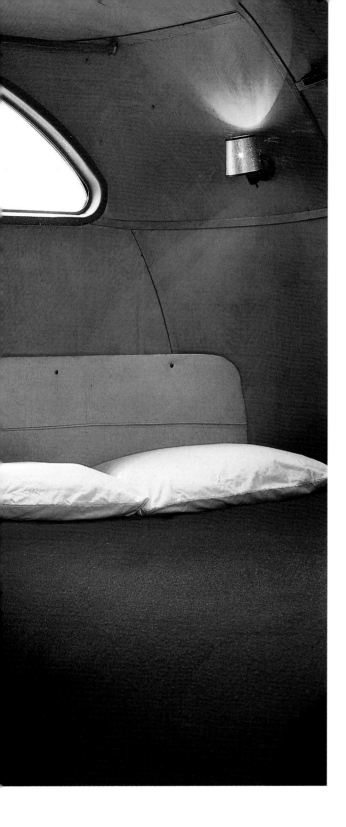

A BEDROOM IN ONE ROUNDED END OF THE TRAILER has curved wood paneling and great lines. The trailer works as part of the cabin because it's very tight and compact and makes great use of all available space.

MODERNIST MASTER

Marcel Breuer was part of the Bauhaus, the legendary German design school founded in 1919 by Walter Gropius where modernism—design for twentieth-century living that purposefully integrated art, crafts, and technology—was first formulated and taught. After the Nazis closed the school in 1933, Breuer and others fled to America. In the 1950s, their modernist vision, known as the International Style, spread around the world.

MODERNISM INTEGRATES ART, CRAFTS, AND TECHNOLOGY INTO DESIGNS FOR TWENTIETH-CENTURY LIVING.

Breuer, who started out as an interior designer, is perhaps best known for the Wassily chair he designed in 1925. It was one of the first pieces to use a steel tube structure, which was strung with leather strips. In the 1930s, Breuer's attention turned to architecture; and in 1937, he joined Gropius at Harvard University and went into partnership with him, creating some of the first modernist buildings in America in the 1940s.

His residential work reveals his interest in natural materials, especially stone and wood.

Rescuing a Heritage

LOG CABINS ARE UNIQUE in their ability to be cataloged, dismantled, transported, and reassembled at another site, which is often how new log structures are created. Nationally known watercolorist Bob Timberlake understood that when he discovered an eighteenth-century cabin about to be demolished in rural Davison County, North Carolina.

Bob liked the idea of reconstructing the primitive cabin on land he owned 10 miles away near Lexington, North Carolina, amid other old structures he has saved from the wave of progress. Over the years, Bob has assembled such an impressive collection of buildings to paint as his nostalgic subject matter that his property has become a sort of outdoor museum.

When Timberlake moved the cabin to his enclave, he added a new porch and dormer. He also remodeled the interior, adding a bathroom and kitchen wing, plus a new stone fireplace. Now, appropriately scaled to his hamlet of buildings, he uses it as a guest house.

"The beauty of a handcrafted log home is that it is timeless," says Bob. "Whether newly completed or a landmark, a handcrafted log home is a link to our past—a part

THE BEDROOM DORMERS SHOW OFF THEIR TIMBER framing, which contrasts nicely with the plastered walls. The scale of the small dormer fits perfectly with the overall scale of the cabin, which is cozy and intimate.

THE RESURRECTED CABIN, WHICH IS ATTACHED TO A FIELDSTONE WALL, has a stone base and kitchen addition made of stone, connecting it in a timeless way to the North Carolina landscape.

AN OLD PINE DOOR LEADS TO A STEEP STAIR-WAY and to the small bedroom above. The hardware on the stair door is hand-forged, in keeping with the hand-crafted look and texture of the rest of the cabin.

of our heritage—a symbol that sets us aside as Americans. Log homes represent all that is good in this country—independence, self-sufficiency, the values of friendship—and the importance of family."

Timberlake repeated the log cabin–saving exercise for several friends. In the process he realized these rustic, historic structures were revered, just like his paintings. A master of merchandizing his brand name, also attached to furniture, clothing, pottery, and other artifacts, he hooked up with Hearthstone log home building company to create the Bob Timberlake Log Home Collection, which ranges from modest to grand log havens.

THE WINDOWS ARE HAND-FLOATED GLASS PANES set in pine frames to approximate the look of the windows in the original structure built in the 1780s. Authenticity was the goal wherever possible. The door leads to a closet tucked under the stairs.

BOB TIMBERLAKE ATTACHED a new but rustic-looking kitchen to the back of the cabin.

THE ORIGINAL OWNERS probably didn't have time to adorn the cabin with a cheery flower box. This planter contrasts nicely with the hand-hewn square oak logs and white chinking.

A SETTLEMENT OF OLD STRUCTURES

Bob Timberlake bought 70 acres of rolling farmland near Lexington, North Carolina, in 1985 and moved a large circa-1809 carriage barn to the property, which became his art studio. He placed the small guest cabin nearby, at one end of an old stone wall. At the other end are other old buildings he renovated.

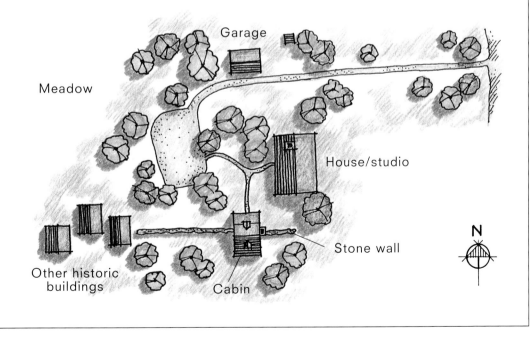

Garage

Meadow

House/studio

Stone wall

Other historic buildings

Cabin

N

RECYCLED DESIGNS

Hearthstone began restoring log homes in 1971. Success soon meant demand exceeded supply, and the company added new log construction, along with timberframing, to its repertoire. Relying on the heritage and tradition of history, Hearthstone eventually became an industry leader in building new homes that look like 150- to 200-year-old log structures.

Working for years on his own, Bob Timberlake created a collection of recycled cabins for himself and friends. More recently, Bob joined forces with Hearthstone, making his work available to a broader, appreciative audience. Hearthstone's Bob Timberlake Log Home Collection has a number of different styles, including The Watkins, a replica of a two-story log cabin with a porch originally built in the early 1800s; The Grove, a three-story flat log cabin modeled after one in Lexington, North Carolina; and The Guest House, which is featured here.

CREATING A HISTORIC CABIN

FIRST FLOOR

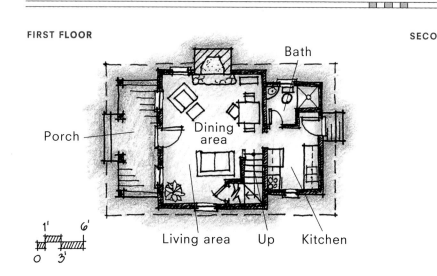

Porch

Dining area

Living area   Up   Kitchen

Bath

1'   6'
0   3'

SECOND FLOOR

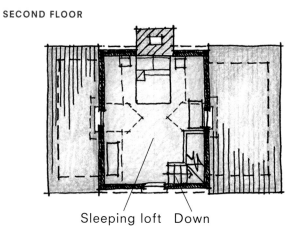

Sleeping loft   Down

A COZY BEDROOM NESTLES UNDER THE GABLE ROOF on the second floor. Cross dormers and a gable-end window provide ample ventilation and morning light.

the Traditional Cabin

STANDARD WAYS OF BUILDING reflect the value of the tried and true. The simple rectilinear building with a gable roof represents a common cultural pattern. Though the traditional cabin is often easily adaptable to technological change and varied layouts, it also retains similarities across North America. However, like any shared language, it includes regional dialects.

Ties to the Land

EOFFREY PRENTISS'S TIES to San Juan Island date back to the 1860s when his great-grandfather homesteaded several hundred acres on the largest of the 176 San Juan Islands that form the border between Canada and Washington State. By 1984 all that remained of the family land was a 2½-acre plot of waterfront property. Because Geoff and his two brothers, who live in Texas and Rhode Island, wanted to maintain a connection to the area, they purchased the land and built a cabin on it so the three families could share vacations.

Though the brothers agreed they wanted a cabin rather than a formal house, Geoff, whose architectural practice is based in Seattle, discovered that designing one structure to meet the very different specifications of the three brothers was no easy task. He devised a detailed questionnaire, modeled on a checklist he found in the book *The Place of Houses,* and then orchestrated a compromise. The cabin is set back from the shoreline on what Geoff calls the "duller part of the site," so the "best spots (like the shore-line) are preserved in their natural beauty." Geoff adds,

ARCHITECT GEOFFREY PRENTISS'S CABIN IS SIMPLE post-and-beam construction, which is common in the San Juan Islands. The basic rectangle is sided with reverse board-and-batten cedar made of roughsawn boards. The cabin's long axis is aligned to take advantage of the solar gain.

BECAUSE THE SLEEPING PORCH ON THE MAIN FLOOR is exposed to the weather on three sides, Geoff installed a waterproof membrane beneath the tongue-and-groove spruce decking so water would not leak into the children's playroom below.

THE HUGE FIREPLACE IS THE FOCAL POINT OF THE CABIN. Constructing it proved to be a puzzle because Geoff had to incorporate a flight of stairs and an outdoor fireplace. First, fireboxes were laid; then flues, intricately positioned around steps, were installed. Once the concrete was poured and had cured, it was belt-sanded to give it a satin-smooth finish.

BECAUSE THE BEDROOM ON THE EASTERN END of the cabin faces the water, Geoff made it small. Then he added an additional 4 ft. of space to the western bedroom, which doesn't have a water view.

A VIEW TO THE SAN JUANS

This 2½-acre piece of waterfront property has been in the Prentiss family since the 1860s. The cabin is a few hundred yards from the shore, though close enough to see the water and hear the waves hit the rocks.

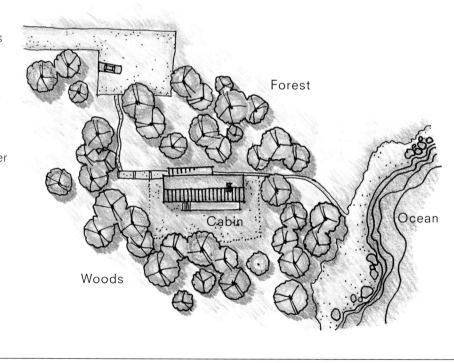

"We still have a view of the water, and you can hear the sound of seals on the rocks below."

The cabin is a large 16-ft. by 60-ft. rectangle, laid out in a grid of 8-ft.-sq. bays with an extra half-bay at the western end. It contains a large central space with a fireplace at one end and a kitchen at the other. All interior and exterior spaces open directly into the central space. To emphasize the number "3", three sets of French doors open onto the deck, and there are three main sleeping areas, two on opposite ends of the second floor and a sleeping porch that has an outdoor fireplace on the first floor.

Geoff, who in the meanwhile became sole owner of the cabin, uses it at least twice a month. Because he does a lot of work in the San Juan Islands, he stays over when meeting clients and doing site visits and often spends weekends there. "I sit in the middle of the main room," he says, "listening to wind, rain, or birds and use the quiet and the beauty to help me design projects."

CAMPING OUT INDOORS

Picture a large, open space—basically a barn—in which people can camp out. Although this cabin encloses such a barnlike space, thanks to its post-and-beam construction, it's actually much more intimate than its openness suggests.

Post-and-beam structures are composed of a series of "bents," or sections of posts connected by beams. In this cabin, there are seven bents, which create six living bays. At each end is a bedroom loft with stairs. **A LARGE, OPEN SPACE IS MORE INTIMATE WHEN SECTIONED OFF AT EACH END.** Under one loft is the kitchen; under the other is a sleeping porch and a fireplace that drives up through the bedroom. That leaves two bays in the middle. Although it's a large, open space, sectioning it off at each end creates a more intimate space in the middle.

LOFTS OPEN ONTO EACH END OF THE CABIN. The kitchen and bathroom (behind the door) are tucked beneath the western end of the cabin so all plumbing can be clustered in the same area. Metal rods suspend shelves from the ceiling.

A TOTAL OF 360 SQUARE PANES OF GLASS enliven the transition between inside and outside. Geoff was inspired, he says, by what "someone sees while moving through the woods, catching glimpses of objects through the random openings between trunks and branches."

A POST-AND-BEAM CABIN

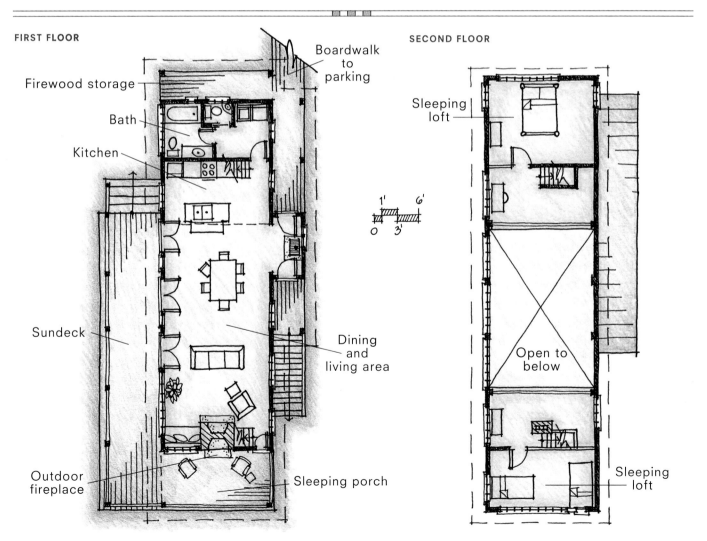

FIRST FLOOR

Boardwalk to parking

Firewood storage

Bath

Kitchen

Sundeck

Outdoor fireplace

Dining and living area

Sleeping porch

SECOND FLOOR

Sleeping loft

Open to below

Sleeping loft

Log Cabin with a View

MONTANA'S FLATHEAD VALLEY IS ONE of the most picturesque natural areas in North America. Still pristine and secluded, the land is fed by streams and springs and surrounded by pungent lodgepole pine, tamarack, and cedar. All that beauty is what attracted Gina and Don—a Canadian couple who enjoy skiing in the winter and fishing in the summer—to buy a chunk of land behind a stretch of shorefront on one of the lakes.

The couple knew they wanted a large shorefront home to accommodate their seven children, who often visit with their growing families; but first they needed a major access road and a bridge over a nearby creek so trucks could bring in the large logs. While that was being done, they decided to construct a small 26-ft. by 36-ft. cabin, christened "The Homestead," which could one day be converted to a guest cabin. They hired Kibo Group Architecture in Missoula to design the cabin and Bill Hart of Hart Builders, Inc., in Whitefish, Montana, a distributor of Rocky Mountain Log Homes, to construct it using 12-ft. spruce logs.

NESTLED AMID A STAND OF OLD-GROWTH TREES overlooking a Montana lake, this log cabin feels like a tree house. The logs were preassembled at the log yard to ensure the proper fit, reassembled on site, and chinked with an expanding grouting material. Because the handcrafted logs taper from one end to the other, they are set in opposing courses to create a traditionally rustic look.

THE COVERED, WRAPAROUND DECK offers spectacular views of the lake during all seasons, though Gina and Don especially enjoy sitting outside, day and evening, during the summer months.

THOUGH THE CABIN'S DESIGN IS TRADITIONAL, floor-to-ceiling glass on the lake side gives the great room an expansive, contemporary look and provides a dramatic view through the deck and log trusses to the lake beyond.

BUILDING THE GUEST CABIN FIRST

Brisk streams, snowy mountains, and the Flathead Valley are the backdrop for this site in northwest Montana. The land was purchased as the site of a getaway big enough for a couple and their seven children. But before the main house was constructed down on the water, the couple built this small cabin up the hill beside the stream.

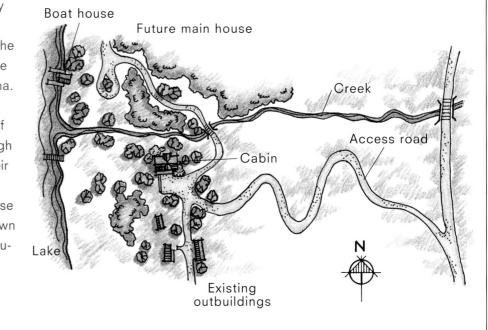

Boat house

Future main house

Creek

Access road

Cabin

Lake

N

Existing outbuildings

One prerequisite was for a large fireplace that didn't obstruct the view. Kibo accommodated by placing the huge stone fireplace on the wall at right angles to the doors and windows facing the deck that overlooks the lake. So the hearth and the view share equal billing, and the cabin is filled with sunlight, even in winter.

Because the cabin is essentially one large room, with the bathroom and an open kitchen on the wall opposite the view, Gina decided to divide it into three separate spaces: a sitting area in front of the hearth, a writing area with table and chairs nearest the deck, and a dining area. The couple sleeps in a loft that overlooks the downstairs room; the loft has a tiny balcony that looks out on a stream.

Though Gina and Don have to drive five hours from Calgary to their getaway cabin, they never mind the trek. There's so much to look forward to when they get there.

GINA POSITIONED AN ANTIQUE WRITING DESK and two hickory chairs near the deck to take advantage of the ample light reflected off the lake. The area also doubles as a reading nook. Small lamps are positioned to define the different areas in the great room.

THE LARGE STONE FIREPLACE, VIEWED THROUGH THE STAIRCASE leading to the overhead loft, is large enough to warm up chilly Montana evenings but not too big to detract from the view. Local materials were used to build it.

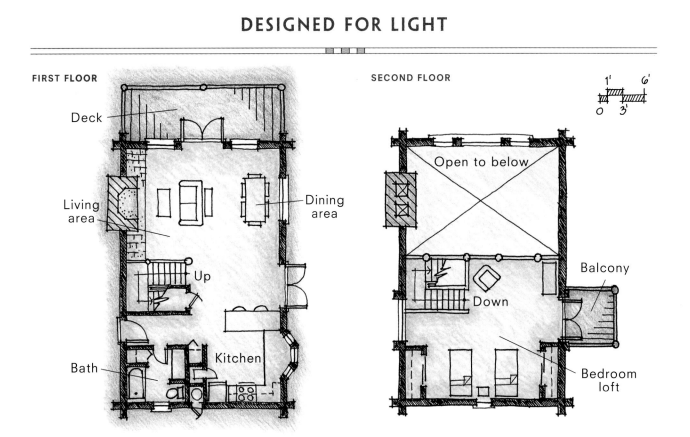

FIRST FLOOR

Deck

Living area

Dining area

Up

Bath

Kitchen

SECOND FLOOR

1' 6'
0 3'

Open to below

Balcony

Down

Bedroom loft

INDIVIDUAL LOGS DETERMINE THE SIZE

The size of available logs often determines the scale and dimension of log buildings. So a modest cabin is frequently one rectangle, whereas a larger log structure contains many rectangles. Commonly, the walls are 13 logs tall. Using logs the size of a standard telephone pole creates a wall that's about 35 ft. high. At least two logs, preferably three, are needed above door height to support the weight of the roof and tie the top of the structure together.

Long logs can be tricky because of their natural taper, which must alternate up the wall—the thick end one way on one course, the other way on the next course. That's the discipline of logs.

THE SIZE OF AVAILABLE LOGS OFTEN DETERMINES THE SCALE AND DIMENSION OF LOG BUILDINGS.

A SLEEPING LOFT COVERS THE BACK THIRD OF THE GREAT ROOM, with the kitchen and bathroom tucked underneath. At the rear of the sleeping loft is a sitting area that leads to a balcony and another beautiful view.

More than the Sum of Its Parts

THIS ENCLAVE—ONLY AN HOUR and a half from home—started as a place where the owner could write poetry, paint, and enjoy calligraphy, a favorite hobby. A ferry ride to it would provide all the mental distance she needed. And the design would carefully shelter views of neighbors, so the open-meadow site could be claimed for solitude.

Christened the "Wren House" by the owner, who is as happy as a wren there, the buildings were constructed over time so their design and siting could respond to whatever evolved. Builder/designer Kim Hoelting was aided by his friend and colleague architect Ross Chapin. Together they collaborated with the client in her search for tranquility.

What has evolved to date includes four components: sleeping, bathing, studio, and garden shed. The sleeping room is clustered with the sauna/bathing area in a sort of Southern dogtrot design united by a common shed roof. They are linked under a canopy to the studio loft so one can travel under cover in the northwestern drizzle. Slightly beyond is the garden shed, scaled to add to the composition of the whole and sited to block views to the neighbors.

THE DIFFERENT ROOF PITCHES OF THE BUILDINGS are noticeable when viewed from the west across the meadow. Like utilitarian agrarian buildings, each is different for a unique architectural reason, but continuity is achieved through materials.

THE TRELLISED WALKWAY CONNECTS THE PRIMARY STRUCTURES so the owner doesn't have to walk in the plentiful Northwest rain. Views along the path are framed north and south by the trellis.

TO TAKE A NAP IN THE LOFT, the owner climbs the ladder over the drawing area. An array of windows and skylights bathes the room in light. Over everything, the fir trim projects a golden glow.

THE BATHING AREA IS AT THE END OF A WOODY HALL. In the background to the right is the shower, which has a skylight that creates an enticing environment.

THE KNOTTY CEDAR BOARDS SEEM TO WARM the sleeping room. The beam-and-purlin ceiling adds a sense of structure and support to the room and visually complements the window view.

The architecture of the buildings is simple: traditional, local forms, each with particular roof pitches. They are unified through their color, use of natural wood, and simple utilitarian windows. The modest scale of the structures makes for an intimate place, a feeling that is further enhanced inside, where these small structures are subdivided into even smaller spaces for drawing and sleeping. Even in the bathing area, functions are separated so each has its own zone. Interiors of drywall and fir trim cast a warm hue while keeping spaces light and cheery in an often gloomy landscape.

DIVIDING UP THE PARTS

It's hard to say which is the most important part of a small, spread-out compound such as this one. Is the heart of it where the owner sleeps? Or is it the studio? Or does it matter? In these forests and meadows of Washington State, all functions seem equal.

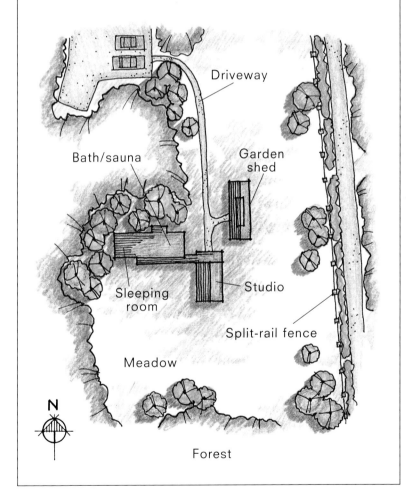

Driveway

Bath/sauna

Garden shed

Sleeping room

Studio

Split-rail fence

Meadow

N

Forest

EVEN A UTILITARIAN GARDEN AND STORAGE SHED can be successfully integrated into a graceful ensemble.

A STRING OF CABINS

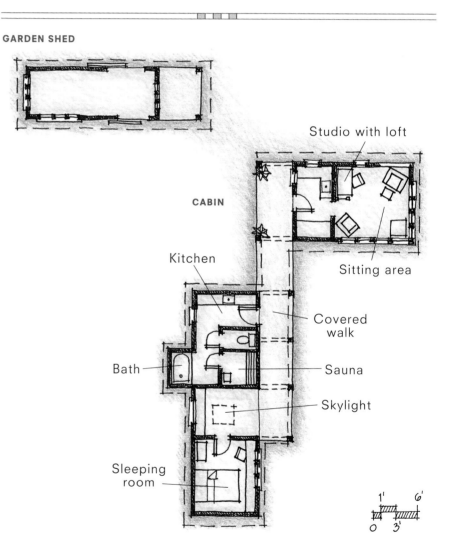

GARDEN SHED

Studio with loft

CABIN

Kitchen

Sitting area

Covered walk

Bath

Sauna

Skylight

Sleeping room

1'   6'
0   3'

A PLACE FOR ONE PERSON IS EXEMPLIFIED BY THE BUILDING SCALE. The porch to the studio provides a gentle place for poetry writing, painting, or sketching the meadow.

A COLLECTION OF SMALL SPACES

The design of several small, intimate structures rather than one larger one can make a place of retreat even better. This design strategy can be seen both here and in the Curtis cabin (see p. 72). For different reasons, each design includes small structures: The Wren House is connected by trellised walkways; the Curtis cabin is strung out along a Lake Superior cliff.

This design strategy promotes outdoor living because one is forced to move between structures and thus honors the site for which the cabin was selected. Separate structures also accommodate individuals who require private space away from family or colleagues for repose or for some specific activity, such as that provided by a painting studio.

This type of enclave was common to hamlets in New England and northern Europe and is still in use today by African tribes on the Serengeti Plain. Modest, incremental construction gives these places a very human scale that's in close touch with nature.

Do-It-Yourself from a Kit

THE CABIN SITS IN THE MIDDLE OF 10 ACRES OF FARM-LAND in a historic preserve established by the National Park Service nearly 15 years ago. Peg Snyder and Michael Mortenson chose the post-and-beam structure because it would blend in with the surrounding farms and age well with the surroundings.

SEATTLE RESIDENTS PEG SNYDER AND MICHAEL MORTENSON knew they wanted a cabin near a farm, with a view of both water and mountains. After looking for property throughout the summer of 1990, they finally snapped up a plot of land that met all their criteria on the 10-acre Colonel Crockett Farm, which dates to the 1860s, on Washington's Whidbey Island.

While camping on the land, they researched the possibilities of what Michael, who had some remodeling experience, could build himself—something that would be affordable and relatively easy to construct. In 1995, a kit for a 24-ft. by 32-ft. barn-shaped structure made by Shelter-Kit in Tilton, New Hampshire, was unloaded off a flatbed truck. Michael and two friends constructed the cabin shell over a three-week vacation.

Snyder and Mortenson, after first developing a plan that suited their needs, worked with the manufacturer so that all the framing pieces were precut to size. The only thing Michael had to cut was the exterior siding. Michael hired a local craftsman to make the windows from salvaged and new materials. To help convey the idea of a

COMMANDING VIEWS

From where it sits, this cabin commands views of both earth and water, from the vantage point of a lovely field of clover. In the summer, the surrounding fields can obscure the views from ground level; but in fall, when all is mowed down, they add a texture to the scene that is breathtakingly beautiful.

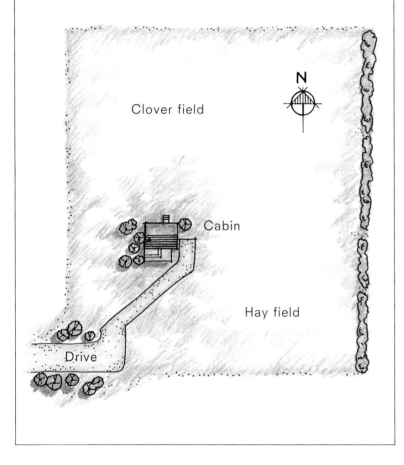

A POST-AND-BEAM STRUCTURE LIKE THIS ONE is naturally divided into sections by the arrangement of beams and their supporting posts. The tiled, raised hearth supports the cast-iron stove, which is set a safe distance from the French doors that open to the deck.

barn, Michael bought some garage doors from the 1920s, removed the middle panel, and rebuilt them to resemble barn doors, which he added to both ends of the cabin. Once the shell was complete, the family, which by then included two small boys, used the cabin as if it were a large tent.

Although it took Michael several more years to finish the interior, he notes that the cabin won't be officially completed until he adds stairs to the sleeping loft over the west end. "Even though we did take five years to complete the house, it really didn't take a lot of time or skill," he says. And who's counting anyway. The family's had all this time to enjoy the view of Puget Sound with the mountains in the distance.

SIMPLE TRIM AND INTERIOR DETAILS keep everything inside the cabin feeling clean and uncluttered so nothing spoils the view through the French doors to Puget Sound.

PUTTING TOGETHER THE NUMBERED PIECES

People who wouldn't dream of building their own home will undertake construction of their own cabin. And often it's a kit that makes the construction possible. The kit provides the map, or the template, of what goes where.

IF YOU CAN PUT A BICYCLE TOGETHER, YOU CAN BUILD A CABIN FROM A KIT.

People think of it this way: You were able to figure out how to put together a bicycle for your children, so a modest 24-ft. by 32-ft. structure should be attainable.

A lot of people like to have a project for their vacations—they don't want to sit still—and building a cabin is such a project. They can get enough done during a vacation to see some real progress on the cabin. Afterward, when they invite friends to the cabin, there's that good sense of "we made this."

LIKE A MODIFIED BARN

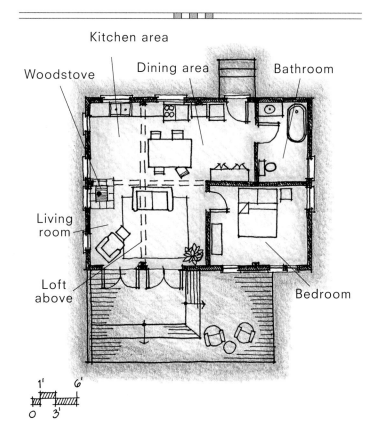

Kitchen area
Dining area
Woodstove
Bathroom
Living room
Loft above
Bedroom

1' 6'
0 3'

PEG AND MICHAEL SPENT MANY HOURS walking the land to find the perfect site for the cabin, which was customized from a kit. The surrounding grounds provide a huge playground for children and adults alike.

THE BASIC COLORS COMPLEMENT THE BASIC DESIGN OF THE CABIN. In the kitchen area, everything is clean and simple, from the painted floor to the layout of cabinets, sink, and appliances.

Cabin out Back

KRISTINA LINDBERGH HAD TO HAVE A WRITER'S CABIN. They are a tradition in her family. Her grandfather Charles Lindbergh built them for her grandmother Anne wherever they lived. So when her brother, Lars, a carpenter, and her sister-in-law, Annette, an architect-trained builder, were living in the old carriage house on her property in rural Westchester County, New York, Kristina commissioned them to build a retreat in the woods about 100 yd. behind her house.

Annette rejected a site closer to the house, because it wouldn't provide enough solitude. So she walked the wooded land until "the site pulled like a magnet. It sat high up among the boulders, and there were no trees I had to cut." She took inspiration for its design from her Scandinavian background and modeled the cabin on a traditional 12-ft. by 12-ft. square, capped with a gable roof. To have minimal impact on the site and yet protect the building from ground moisture, she had concrete footings put in and set the structure on pressure-treated 6-in. by 6-in. piers, rather than flat on a poured foundation.

THE WOOD USED FOR THE PORCH COLUMNS AND RAILINGS is abundant local ash. Taken from standing dead trees on the property, hardwood ash resists rot, although builder Annette Lindbergh had the column ends dipped in water sealer for extra protection. The branches used for the balusters were taken from the tops of beech trees.

THE WINDOWS, RECYCLED FROM THE OLD CARRIAGE HOUSE on the property, were completely renovated by carpenter Lars Lindbergh before he installed them in the cabin. The writer's desk is positioned in front of the rear window to provide maximum inspiration—or infinite distraction.

THE CABIN'S PRIMARY COLORS WERE INSPIRED by traditional Scandinavian architecture, as were its diamond-shaped window and the decorative detail over the porch. Although the area was hilly and strewn with large boulders, Annette was able to construct the tiny cabin on a level foundation by raising it up on wooden piers set on poured concrete bases.

To maximize the interior space and expand the cabin's usefulness, Annette designed a sleeping loft that extends over the front porch. Not wanting to put up drywall because it's susceptible to mildew, Annette had Lars panel the interior walls with pine planks. In fact, Lars did all the interior carpentry, recycling windows from the old carriage house and laying down wide plank flooring that was salvaged when Kristina's kitchen was remodeled. The cabin is fully insulated, electrified, and has a phone line.

Although Kristina wishes she could spend more time writing there, her children make frequent use of the cabin. During the day it's a playhouse; at night it's ideal for sleepovers. Annette found the project so rewarding that she turned it into a business. Through her company, Tiny Houses Inc., she builds cabins and restores small structures all over Westchester County.

TO PUT THE SPACE NEAR THE RAFTERS TO GOOD USE, Annette built a loft over the front door. The resulting sleeping space, although not high enough for an adult to stand at full height, is wide enough to sleep three or four, which makes it perfect for slumber parties.

SETTLED AMONG ROCKS AND TREES

Only 100 yd. from the main house, this little cabin sits in a boulder-strewn area in the dense woods of rural Upstate New York. With forest all around, the site was perfect for the cabin. It has a solid foundation, and no clearing was necessary to build it.

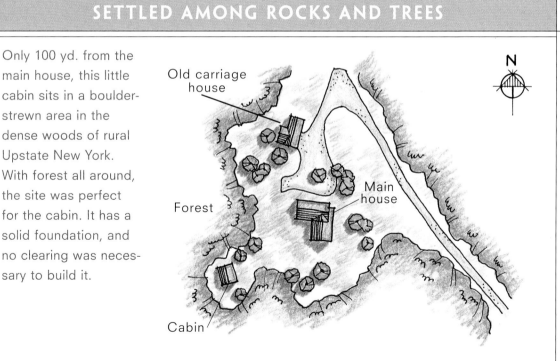

N

Old carriage house

Forest

Main house

Cabin

WRITERS' RETREATS

Going to a secluded cabin to write is a prized practice among writers. Playwright Eugene O'Neill is reported to have written some of his earliest plays in a weather-beaten cabin facing the ocean in Provincetown, on Cape Cod.

Some writers have built cabins for themselves. Henry David Thoreau is probably the most famous in this category. He built a one-room cabin in Concord, Massachusetts, and lived in it for a year and a half, storing up experiences he would later develop into *Walden*. In 1949, playwright Arthur Miller built an one-room cabin a short distance from his home in Connecticut where he wrote *Death of a Salesman*.

There is something special about the private peacefulness and close connection with nature that a cabin offers writers. "It's heavenly to go up to the cabin to write," says Kristina Lindbergh, following in her grandmother Anne Morrow Lindbergh's footsteps. "Whenever I go up there, I feel like I'm in a different world."

A WRITER'S TINY GETAWAY

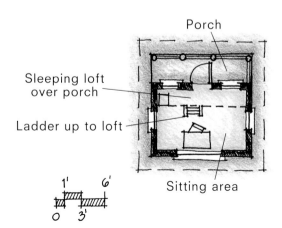

Porch

Sleeping loft over porch

Ladder up to loft

Sitting area

1'   6'
0   3'

LARS PANELED THE WALLS WITH PINE and made the floor from planks recycled from Kristina Lindbergh's original kitchen. An old library ladder is always in position to provide easy access to the loft.

Paradise on a Budget

JIM HATTORI AND LISA PETERS, a young Seattle professional couple passionate about cross-country skiing and mountain biking, found the perfect place to practice their sports in northern Washington State's Methow Valley. They asked Seattle architect Thomas Lawrence to build them a modest cabin for vacations and long weekends that would give them easy access to the land and great views of the surrounding valley.

Because of a limited budget, the spectacular site, and the modest requests of his clients, Thomas opted for restraint. He sited the cabin on the 3-acre lot to frame the best views and to catch the prevailing breezes. Then he chose an elongated plan with a conventional gabled roof to give the building some presence within its land-scape on the eastern side of the Cascade Mountains. The encircling porch provides a buffer from weather extremes, shading most windows in the summer and providing a snow-free area during the winter. The exposed round wooden piers on the porch make the building appear to float lightly over the land.

WHEN THEY'RE NOT CYCLING, THE COUPLE spends a lot of time sitting on the wide porch. "Because the porch surrounds the cabin, we alternate where we sit, depending on the wind and sun," says Jim Hattori. The porch also comes in handy during the winter for storing skis.

SITTING IN THE MIDST OF A 3-ACRE SITE, the cabin looks and feels isolated. Though the cabin is part of a planned development, it will remain secluded, because it borders a large tract that will never be developed.

Designed for low maintenance, the interior has one large open room downstairs for eating, cooking, and lounging, with a loft that contains two separate office areas for the busy couple and a small sleeping area for friends. A utility room/mudroom was designed so the couple would have plenty of space for waxing their skis.

ALTHOUGH THE CABIN IS A SIMPLE RECTANGLE, its expansive porch on all four sides and sharply gabled roof give the cabin elegant, classic lines. Using board-and-batten cedar siding and a standing-seam metal roofing, architect Thomas Lawrence created a relatively inexpensive retreat in 1995 for $75 per square foot.

JIM HATTORI AND LISA PETERS SELECTED THE SITE for their Methow Valley cabin because of the views and its proximity to groomed cross-country ski trails, which are just 100 yd. from the porch. They also wanted a flat site to make it more accessible during snowy winters.

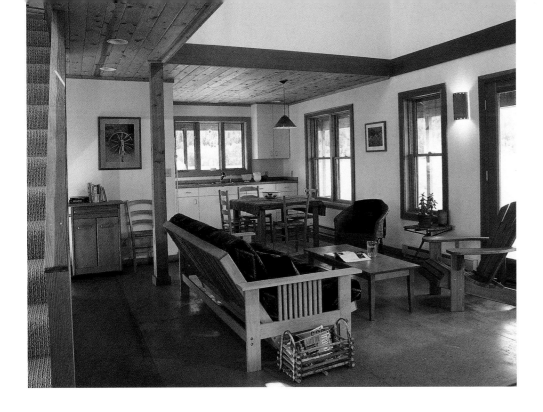

THE MAIN LIVING AREA IS OPEN AND INFORMAL, with clear-finished wood floors, prefabricated plastic-laminate kitchen cabinets, fir doors, and energy-efficient, aluminum-clad pine windows. The arrangement of windows and the orientation of the house ensure good cross-ventilation in the summer, when temperatures can reach 100°F.

DOWN IN THE VALLEY

Being just off a main road makes the cabin easy to access during the winter, when the owners visit for cross-country skiing. The 3-acre site sits in the middle of an open valley, so the wrap-around porch offers views of the Methow River Valley and of the spectacular Cascade Mountain range to the west.

Grasslands

Drive

View to mountains

Cabin

N

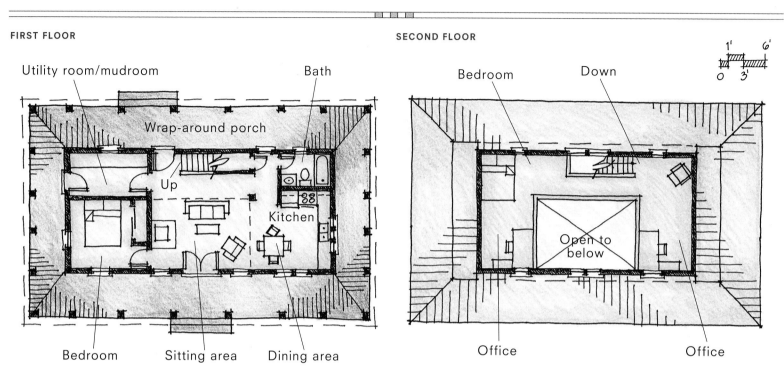

FIRST FLOOR

Utility room/mudroom

Bath

Wrap-around porch

Up

Kitchen

Bedroom

Sitting area

Dining area

SECOND FLOOR

Bedroom

Down

Open to below

Office

Office

A ROOF LIKE A COWBOY HAT

"What originally attracted us to this cabin is its shape, which, like a hat, forms a shelter to protect people in this big landscape. It doesn't try to hide. It doesn't hunker down next to a hill. It's out in the wide-open valley. And it seems to lift up into the sky to grab the views from the second level, while the ground level is even with the landscape, so people there can be part of the view."

WHETHER GETTING UP AT SUNRISE OR SETTLING IN AT SUNSET, PEOPLE HAVE A PLACE OUTSIDE TO ENJOY NATURE.

It is significant that people can walk out on all sides and that each elevation has a porch that offers a great view. So whether people are getting up at sunrise or settling in at sunset, there is a place outside to enjoy nature, either sitting in the sun on a wintry day or hiding from the sun on a blistering day.

FINDING A WOODSTOVE SUITED TO THE SPIRIT of the modern cabin was a challenge, because most woodstoves are based on historic styles. This well-made stove had a look that pleased the owners and came with a glass door that allows the couple to watch the fire. The bedroom is to the left of the stove, and the utility room/mudroom is on the right.

Wilderness Wonderland

IMAGINE A GIFT OF 113 ACRES of Montana wilderness. After a neighbor deeded that to Jeff and Lois Shelden for $2 in 1993, they began walking their long, narrow stretch of land in the Judith Mountains looking for a place to build a cabin to replace the dark and damp existing one. After a forest fire raged out of control one autumn, it exposed the view from a long rocky rib of limestone that climbs to the top of a mountain.

They decided to build the cabin halfway up the ridge where there's lots of open space and they wouldn't have to worry about their kids playing near a cliff. Not having to build a road, which would be costly and would scar the land, was another consideration. In the summer, the family drives to the cabin on a jeep trail; from November to mid-April the area becomes wilderness, so they ski in a half mile from a paved county road.

Jeff, who practices architecture in Lewistown, Montana, designed the cabin with windows all around the upper story like a lookout tower for two reasons: Lois wanted the cabin to be filled with light, and Jeff wanted to replicate the lookout towers he used to visit when his

THE CABIN SITS PARTWAY UP A RIDGE in Alpine Gulch in Montana's Judith Mountains. Designed to resemble a lookout tower, the cabin was built with local stone and wood recycled from an abandoned railroad line in Utah. The metal roof, salvaged from an old barn, has a generous overhang to shelter the redwood deck below. The owners installed a solar-driven photovoltaic system on the back roof (one sunny winter's day charge supplies three days' power) that furnishes all the cabin's electrical needs.

forester dad took him on field trips as a kid. Jeff subcontracted all the masonry work to Bob Valach and the heavy timber, dimensional framing, and exterior finish work to Bud Barta. He did all the interior finish, plumbing, insulation, electrical work, and landscaping himself, a project that took two years.

Most of the wood was recycled from an abandoned railroad line built across the Great Salt Lake: all the heavy timbers (old-growth fir) from a trestle, the exterior redwood deck and trim from old railroad ties, and the second-floor flooring from former pilings. The corrugated metal roof was salvaged from a nearby barn, and the rock on the lower floor was gathered from land about 2 miles away.

Because it is only 17 miles from their home, the Shelden family uses the cabin often, sometimes just for a Sunday afternoon or an evening cookout. They tend to stay longer—maybe two or three days—in the winter.

TO MAXIMIZE THE LIGHT ON THE UPPER FLOOR, Jeff Shelden designed a 6-ft.-sq. pyramidal skylight at the peak. Though barely noticeable from the outside, the skylight reveals the structural grid on the interior. "It lets a lot of light in—per my wife's requirements—and you can also see the rain or the snow or the stars," he says.

THE VIEW PROVIDES MOST OF THE VISUAL FOCUS on the 14-ft., 8-in.-sq. upper floor, which is simply furnished out of the L.L. Bean catalog. The woodstove in one corner, which was a gift from Jeff's father, provides necessary heat through most of the year. The height of the cabin from the tip of the pyramid to the ground floor is 24½ ft.

COMFORT IN A SEVERE CLIMATE

The land is rugged and steep and the winters are hard. All around is dense Montana mountain wilderness. Yet rising above the harsh and beautiful natural world is this cabin, perched on a limestone ledge and fitted out with all the comforts of home, including a hot tub.

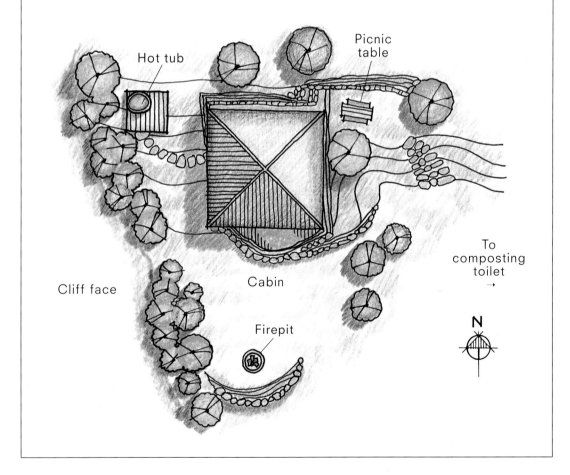

Hot tub

Picnic table

To composting toilet →

N

Cliff face

Cabin

Firepit

MOUNTAIN ICON

The Montana mountains are dotted with lookout towers—simple shelters several stories high that are open all around—that were built by the U.S. Forest Service to enable foresters to survey the area and spot forest fires. The towers have exerted such a powerful influence on people living in the state that they inspired two of the Montana cabins in this book (see p. 244).

Architect Jeff Shelden wanted to evoke the mystique of an old lookout tower—"one like the CCC [Civilian Conservation Corps] might have constructed back in the 1930s"—in homage to his forester father whom he used to accompany on field trips at age 10 or 11. "A lot of those trips involved stops at lookout towers—even an occasional night in one," recalls Jeff. "Lookouts came to seem like romantic, ideal places from which to view the world. They always seemed so exotic to me, perched on a rocky ledge somewhere, subject to the wind and the lightning. Everything about life seemed reduced to its basic elements—except for the expansive views."

Though many lookout towers are no longer used by the Forest Service, they can be rented by people seeking the unique experience of viewing vast vistas of the Montana wilderness from their towering heights.

A TOWERING VIEW

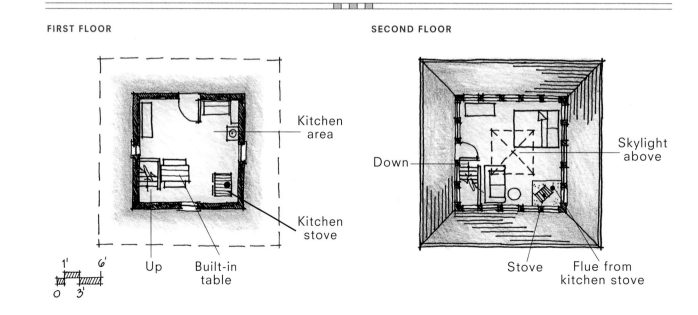

FIRST FLOOR

SECOND FLOOR

Kitchen area

Kitchen stove

Up

Built-in table

Down

Skylight above

Stove

Flue from kitchen stove

THE LOWER FLOOR IS MADE OF TAN QUARTZITE QUARRIED IN IDAHO. Jeff had the stone custom-cut into 8-in. by 8-in. squares to reflect the grid of the ceiling beams. He picked the color of the flooring—and that for the walls above the wainscoting—to match the antique enameled stove. Instead of built-in cabinets, a Hoosier kitchen sits in one corner.

JEFF DESIGNED THE DINING TABLE ON THE LOWER FLOOR and attached it to the wall to maximize floor space in the 14½-ft.-sq. area. The wall behind the table contains the entryway, with built-in storage on the other side. The white wainscot siding is 1x4 tongue-and-groove paneling, which the local mill calls "ceiling board." Jeff used it for the ceilings on both floors.

The Better to See the Water

AS IT GOT HARDER AND HARDER for William and Wilder Witt to find suitable campsites for themselves and their growing children, William, an architect, thought it was time to build the family a cabin. After scouring the area within a two-hour radius of their Seattle home, the couple found a modest site on a secluded lagoon in the Ebys Landing National Historic District of Whidbey Island. It had the advantage of waterfront property without the waterfront price. The family also liked that the island gets a quarter of the rainfall of Seattle so they could enjoy the outdoors more often than they could in the city.

Even though the site seemed to have plenty of room, the septic system took up so much of the property that Bill decided to set the cabin to one side, just a few yards from the waterfront, next to a beautiful old madrona tree. To provide maximum privacy on the site and keep the splendid views of the water, Bill designed the cabin with three floors, each a large, open room. The kids' built-in bunk beds are tucked into alcoves in the front corners of the ground floor, which also has an open sitting area and an outdoor deck. The main floor, which has a balcony,

THE CEILING BEAMS, WINDOW FRAMES, AND FLOORS were left unfinished to create contrast with the brightly painted walls and trim throughout the cabin.

BILL WITT DESIGNED THIS THREE-STORY CABIN as a cube topped with a prism but then broke that shape by making the ground-floor deck pointed like the prow of a ship. The green lattice on the top floor adds inexpensive decoration, providing a vibrant mix of color.

ORIENTED TOWARD THE WATER

Sited on a lagoon in a national historic district of Washington State's Whidbey Island, this three-story cabin sits mere yards from the water, under the broad reach of an old madrona tree. A balcony on the main floor and a deck on the ground floor provide views of the lagoon from the primary living spaces.

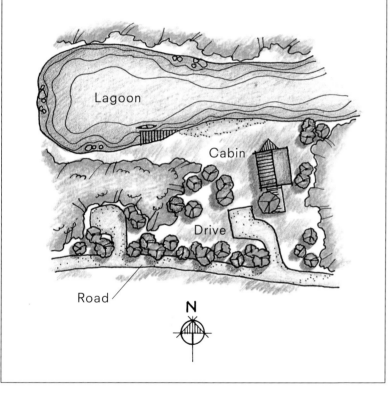

TO MAXIMIZE LIGHT ON THE MAIN FLOOR, Bill designed a large window on one side and a large expanse of glass across the balcony. He chose a dark shade of green for the walls, because the deep color tends to disappear and focus the eye on the views outside.

contains a traditional great room for eating and socializing. And the top floor has the master bedroom and a small office area, with openings on the east and west sides that let light down into the main floor.

Because Bill wanted to construct the cabin as simply and cheaply as possible, he used exterior cedar plywood siding with battens and lattice for decoration and tongue-and-groove decking for floors and ceilings. A dark green shingle roof matches the color of the siding. "Deep green and burgundy red are traditional cabin colors that we saw in the area," notes Bill. "We combined them and added a few turquoise accents. The colors are quite rich, yet because they are deep they make the cabin blend in with the woods."

MANY BUILT-IN FEATURES IN THE CABIN make efficient use of the limited space, such as the kids' bunk beds and work areas on the ground floor. "It's a little like a boat," Bill says. With the children's room on the ground floor and the parents' room on the top, the three-story cabin provides maximum privacy when the family is alone or when there are guests.

POINTED LIKE THE PROW OF A SHIP

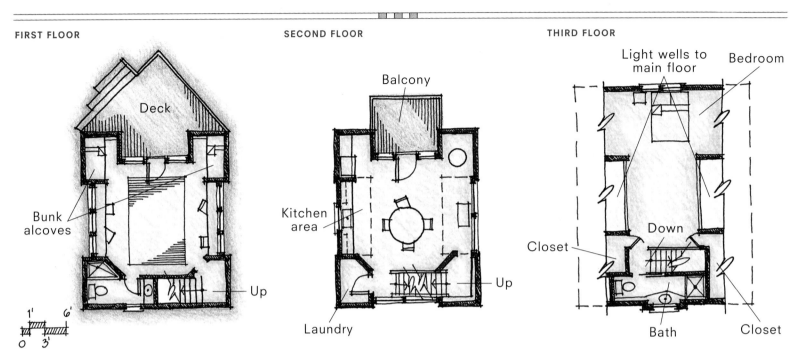

FIRST FLOOR

Deck

Bunk alcoves

Up

1' 6'
0 3'

SECOND FLOOR

Balcony

Kitchen area

Up

Laundry

THIRD FLOOR

Light wells to main floor

Bedroom

Closet

Down

Bath

Closet

FINDING THE RIGHT SITE

The most important aspect of creating a place of retreat may be finding the right site. It's essential to figure out how you want your getaway to function in your life. What's its purpose? How can it best fulfill your dreams? Try drawing up a list of questions; then work through it until you find answers that satisfy all your wants and needs.

How far away from home do you want to be? Do you want to drive just a few hours? Are you able to travel through a couple of states to reach the cabin? Or do you want to be only a short distance from home?

What kind of terrain appeals to you? Do wide open mountain vistas thrill you, or does nestling in the pines close to a lake suit you better? Do you want a place where you can participate in your favorite sports? Pinpointing the location that inspires, calms, or energizes you is vital.

How do you intend to use the cabin? If it's for weekends year-round, then you'll want a spot close to home. But if you intend to use the cabin for extended vacations, you might be willing to travel farther from home.

THE KITCHEN, WHICH HAS STOCK NATURAL-WOOD CABINETS, is efficiently organized along a side wall of the great room. To add interest, Bill painted the molding above a bright pink with a triangular motif in the center. The interplay of colors in the room creates excitement with minimum expense.

Like Living on a Yacht

WATCH ISLAND IS SUCH A TINY (4,400 sq. ft.) spot in the southeast corner of Oceetah Lake that when Bruce Darring bought it, in 1985, he discovered it didn't fit the Adirondack Park Agency's criteria of a "buildable property," even though the foundation of an old cabin remained. But he was determined to build a cabin there to enjoy the island's unique vista of mountains and sky. During the 24 months he waited for the necessary permits, he landscaped the property, planting 40 trees.

Over the course of the next five years, Bruce, who has been a designer-builder in Saranac Lake, New York, since 1975, designed and built the five small buildings in his island camp. The main problem he encountered was finding a work barge that could carry five tons at a time and still navigate the lake's shallow water.

Bruce solved the basic problems of building on an island by installing solar panels, a wind generator, a battery bank, and an inverter to provide electricity. He also has a small back-up generator, used mostly during construction. Submarine phone lines are used around the lake. To get

BUILDER BRUCE DARRING BROUGHT IN MATERIALS TO CONSTRUCT HIS CAMP in the middle of Oceetah Lake. Exterior siding is made from logs sawn so that bark is left on one edge, a technique that requires careful framing to get good results.

THE WATCH ISLAND CAMP CONSISTS OF THE MAIN CABIN (LEFT), which contains the living room and kitchen; a bunk house with four single beds; Bruce's bedroom cabin, which he calls the "sleeping cabin"; a comfort station, with vanity, shower, and utilities on the first floor and guest bedroom on the second floor; and a privy.

TO CREATE THE SANDSTONE FACADE OF THE FIREPLACE, Bruce built a model, simulating the fireplace in his Saranac Lake shop. He then positioned and numbered each hand-cut stone to make sure it fit before hauling it to the island. Because of bad snow conditions, he and a friend transported all the stones in batches of 15 or 20 using children's plastic sleighs.

THE TWIG WORK WAS INSPIRED BY THE TRADITION of the great camps of the Adirondacks. "During the 1970s I spent time on Upper St. Regis Lake and was inspired by the boathouse of the Post Camp," Bruce relates. "Twig work is indigenous to other wooded, mountainous areas all over the world, not just the Adirondacks."

rid of waste, Bruce installed a gray-water seepage system and an organic composting toilet.

The ongoing problem that Bruce can't solve easily is the height of the water. When it's high, the lake floods the lawn and undermines the buildings; when it's low, it's difficult to navigate the river to get to the island. Beaver and muskrats burrowing into the island create areas that cave in when the water's high.

"Transportation during the winter months is probably the main hardship," says Bruce, who has gotten there via snowmobile, skis, and 10-speed bike. "When all else fails, I walk, but it can be a hassle; and unsafe ice is always a consideration." During boating season it's a 10-minute ride from his slip in town.

The feeling Bruce wanted to create on Watch Island is that "you're on a yacht. You look out at water, not grounds, so it feels very nautical. And the sounds at night are of fish jumping, bald eagles flying overhead, and coyotes howling. It's great being in the middle of the lake—so secluded and private—yet right in front of the high peaks. The sunsets are the best of all time, with a feeling of big sky."

AN ISLAND THE SIZE OF A HOUSE

This cabin and the tiny island it occupies sit like a barge in New York State's Oceetah Lake. At 4,400 sq. ft., Watch Island is so small that it offers commanding views of the nearby Adirondack Mountains from every window in the batch of discrete rooms that make up the little cabin complex. Stacks of railroad cross-tie cribbing reinforce the shoreline of the island.

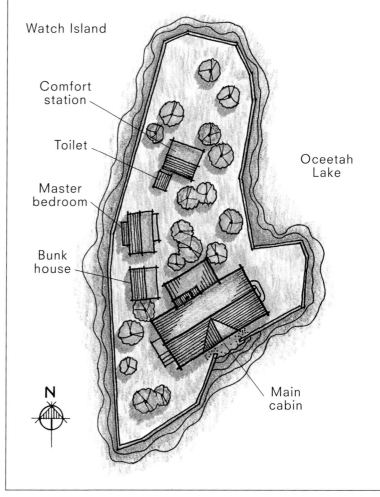

Watch Island

Comfort station

Toilet

Master bedroom

Bunk house

Oceetah Lake

Main cabin

N

THE DOWNS AND UPS OF ISLAND BUILDING

Building on an island is always tricky. First, zoning restrictions for islands are more stringent than those for the mainland. Septic systems are a problem because there's not a lot of soil for a drainage field. And it's often hard to get a well driller out to an island. Of course, you can use lake water for bathing and may be able to use filters for drinking water.

If power lines cannot be placed on the lake bed, you'll have to think about solar- or wind-generated power or a gas-powered generator.

Remember that everything has to be ferried to an island, although a barge service may exist. Premanufactured components are a great way to go, as long as each element is small enough to fit in a boat. That's the downside. The upside is an incredible sense of retreat: You leave the world behind in a unique way.

BRUCE USED MATERIALS HE'D SAVED FROM HIS MILLWORK SHOP, including a number of doors and nine 3-ft. by 7-ft. mahogany windows, originally intended for a New York City brownstone. He incorporated seven different species of wood in the main room: ash, black walnut, cherry, mahogany, oak, pine, and poplar. The ceiling is coffered, with mirrored panels in the center "to pick up a play of light off the water and reflect it around the room."

A FLOATING CABIN FOR LIVING

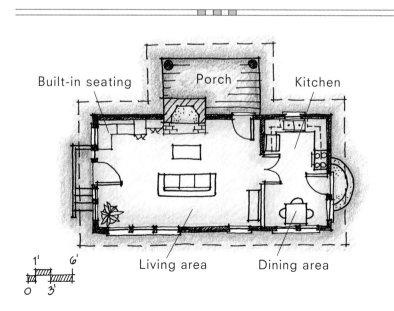

Built-in seating

Porch

Kitchen

Living area

Dining area

1'   6'

O   3'

All You Really Need

THEY ARE ADULTS NOW, but as children Anna and Kira spent weekends and vacations helping to build a cabin that's just a big screened porch and that has, in fact, been dubbed "Le Porch."

Dale and Jan Mulfinger's older daughter, Kira, says, "Friends, family, boyfriends, everyone pitched in. We all built it." Younger daughter, Anna, exclaims, "Then Dad's whole office showed up once each summer for the Karl Marx Regatta, until the crowd got so big they actually broke the dock."

This 14-ft. by 18-ft., east-facing porch one hour away from the Mulfingers' city house in Minneapolis has contributed great lore to the Mulfinger family. It's like going camping without having to remember to bring the tent. In the mid-1980s Dale and Jan found an inexpensive lot on a clean, swimmable lake in Wisconsin. The modest budget of the young family dictated a minimalist structure. They wanted a no-maintenance shelter where a stay at the lake could last hours, days, or even weeks.

SCANDINAVIAN REDS AND BLUES, reflecting the owners' ancestral heritage, decorate this basic structure. Trees filter views to the water and create privacy from the lake.

A WARM GLOW CONNECTS "LE PORCH" WITH THE FIRE PIT OUTSIDE. Located conveniently close to the cabin, the pit is great for wiener roasts and toasting marshmallows. Sheltered by a canopy of deciduous trees, the cabin opens to southern sun and eastern lake views during the day.

THE BASIC REQUIREMENTS OF SHELTER

It's never been locked—that wouldn't be possible. Whatever the temperature outside, it's the same inside. Two sides are always open and can't be closed.

So what are the minimal attributes, or requirements, of a cabin? To keep out the rain and bugs, create space for a few people, and allow room to store a few things. This cabin accomplishes just those basics, up a notch from simple camping. It's built on a concrete slab, not on the dirt; it's permanent so there's no tent to lug. Mostly used for day trips, it's like a picnic shelter at a state park that accommodates up to 10 people. But people can stay overnight, and the family has even stayed there as long as two weeks, cooking on a hotplate or outside on a grill. There's electricity for lighting, and a refrigerator for perishables. And that's about it.

THIS CABIN ACCOMPLISHES THE BASICS, UP A NOTCH FROM SIMPLE CAMPING.

The simple design offers many pluses. A porch is not even an officially habitable structure, so the tax assessor claims. And closing the cabin at the end of summer means just stacking the furniture in the corner, switching off the electrical circuit breaker, and latching the screen door. It takes more effort to haul in the dock.

Anna and Kira reminisce about having felt exposed and naked to nature at Le Porch, but they soon learned that dressing was just a matter of "looking the other way." The hardest adaptation was leaving the confines of warm sleeping bags for a dreaded cool morning stroll to the outhouse. But they didn't complain when they listened to the rain, woke up to the squirrels shadow-dancing across the sunrise, or watched a mother bird teach her newborn to search for worms.

THE LOFT AWAITS SLEEPING BAGS. Morning sunshine awakens sleepers in the loft as it reflects off the lake and onto the red ceiling, which is finished with third-generation recycled silo staves. Ventilation comes from openings to the north.

"LE PORCH" IN THE THICK OF IT

A mere 14 ft. by 18 ft., this cabin resides at the end of a cul-de-sac, facing a small lake in western Wisconsin. Facilities are few—just the necessities: an outhouse, an outdoor grill, and a dock.

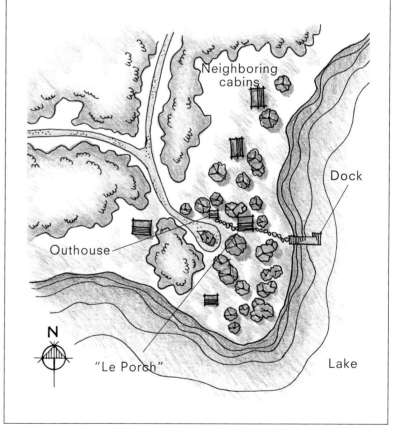

Neighboring cabins

Dock

Outhouse

N

"Le Porch"

Lake

THE BUILT-IN, HINGED, SOLID-CORE DOOR OPENS to create extra sleeping space, using storage cubes as supports for the foot of the bed. By day, the cubes provide extra seating for a family gathering on a warm summer day.

FRESH-AIR RETREAT

THE DOOR FUNCTIONS AS SEATING when it's not used as a bed. Dale salvaged the kitchen cabinets from one of his construction projects. Electrical wires run between the parallel ceiling beams.

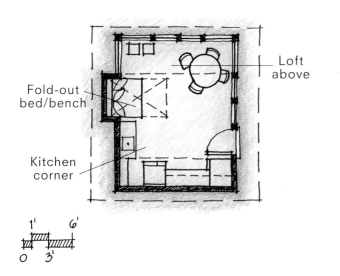

Loft above

Fold-out bed/bench

Kitchen corner

1'   6'

0   3'

Planning a Community

NOT ALL CABINS ARE INDIVIDUAL DESIGNS built for one client on a particular site. Some work just as well as part of an enclave of similar structures. One such development is Quiet Water on the Yachats River, located a short distance from the Oregon coast.

Here, architects Rob Thallon and David Edrington designed an environmentally sensitive community of 32 vacation retreats. Located in a preserved alder grove, the community also shares a swimming pool and tennis and basketball courts. The cabins are built in four clusters of eight, with each unit sharing a public commons while opening to private views of nature and the river beyond. Thus all the cabins have a distinct front and back, with front porches offering social space on the commons and a rear deck overlooking the river.

The cabins, which are similarly laid out, are all deep and narrow, with few side windows for privacy. The living room is open to the second floor, where clerestory windows increase the light below. Window bays in the living room and dining area catch glimpses of the river and provide comfortable sleeping niches. The second-floor sleep-

THOUGH THE EXTERIOR IS EXPRESSED IN SIMPLE plywood and battens, this basic construction did not prevent the project from winning an award of merit from *Sunset* magazine in 1985.

THE MAIN ROOM IS DEEP AND NARROW and open to the second floor. The clerestory windows bring in light that wouldn't reach lower windows. Plywood walls with battens create a rich wooden environment at a relatively low cost. The sleeping nook to the right essentially adds another bed to the cabin.

SHARING THE LAND

Like people in a condominium community, some cabin owners enjoy shared amenities. There are values in such a shared arrangement. In this case, sharing the expense makes waterside property more affordable. Also, there are practical, day-to-day considerations: Everybody knows what color gray stain they need, everybody shares a pool and tennis courts, everybody pays the same amount each month for maintenance and upkeep—and, therefore, everybody can devote more of his retreat time to actual retreating, rather than to mowing, painting, and roofing.

IN A SHARED COMMUNITY, PEOPLE CAN DEVOTE MORE OF THEIR RETREAT TIME TO ACTUAL RETREATING.

ing and bathing rooms are tucked under the roof to enhance the cabin feeling and reduce the exterior scale.

The character of the cabins comes from a combination of simple shapes, good proportions, and warm natural colors that blend nicely with nature. The exterior is plywood with thin, vertical battens in muted gray. The interior features fir plywood walls and fir floors. Interior doors and cabinets are made from fir planks. Windows are a sort of casement and were tailored to the project: As in early American cabins, these are hinged to swing to the inside. Hardware is common farm and gate material in black, which adds a simple rustic character to the interior.

THE KITCHEN, WITH ITS PLAIN OPEN SHELVING and exposed floor joists overhead, gets the job done without much fuss. It's tucked under the sleeping loft. Behind the kitchen is a bathroom.

A CABIN NEIGHBORHOOD

There are all sorts of resort developments, many of them built around water. Some are miniature cities, such as Seaside, Florida. Others, like Quietwater, are less ambitious, more unassuming. In either case, people learn to co-exist with strangers and to share commons areas, waterfront, and the pool.

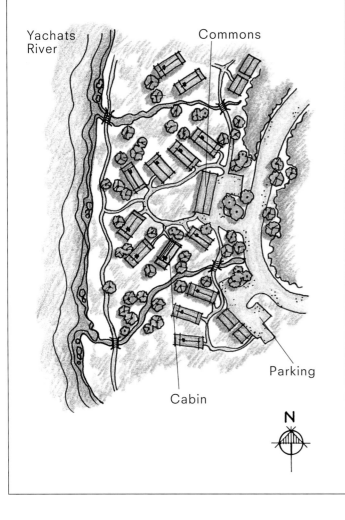

Yachats River

Commons

Parking

Cabin

N

OLD-STYLE CASEMENT WINDOWS THAT SWING INWARD to stay out of the wind and inclement weather contribute to the timeless character of the enclave. Here, the dining table is pushed up to the window seat to create an ad hoc breakfast area.

DISTINCT FRONT AND BACK

FIRST FLOOR

Up

Window seat

Eating area

Deck

Front porch

Bath

Kitchen

Sleeping alcove

Sitting area

1' 6'
0 3'

SECOND FLOOR

Down

Open to below

Bath

Sleeping area

IN THE UPSTAIRS BEDROOM LOFT a bed rests against the cozy kneewall. On the opposite wall a skylight drops light into the loft between his and her closets.

A Better Place to Enjoy Nature

THE OWNERS OF AN EAST COAST ESTATE dreamed of building a large log-cabin lodge that would sleep nearly two dozen; but when the engineers discouraged them, they didn't give up their log cabin dream entirely. Instead, they commissioned Centerbrook architect Mark Simon to build a tiny, playful log cabin not far from the lodge.

Called the Marsh Pavilion by its owners, the cabin is set on a platform raised 4 ft. above the soft, spongy ground so that water can move beneath it as needed. Because the land is part of a floodplain, local authorities had to approve the design to make sure it didn't damage the environment. Custom-built by general contractor E. A. Baker in Takoma Park, Maryland, the prefabricated pine cabin was assembled on site in 1992.

Built high above the floodplain, the cabin rests on tall wooden posts driven 30 ft. to 60 ft. into the marsh. The owners wanted the cabin to function as both indoor and outdoor space so the one-room pavilion is flanked by porches on both ends. The front porch, which is connected to the main lodge by a boardwalk, is meant to be private, or closed. The back porch is meant to be public,

IN KEEPING WITH THE CABIN'S TRADITIONAL BUT MODERN THEME, architect Mark Simon designed an asymmetrical pattern of logs to hold up the porch roof.

THE BACK PORCH ALLOWS MAXIMUM EXPOSURE to the expanse of plants and wildlife that surround the cabin. The porch, set with outdoor furniture, is deep enough to provide shelter from the elements.

THE CABIN BEYOND THE TREES

Like many structures built on wet or marshy ground, this tiny cabin is raised several feet off the ground and set on piers driven deep below the wet ground and into solid soil. Designed for its site, the cabin opens at both ends to take in views of the trees, marsh, and wildlife.

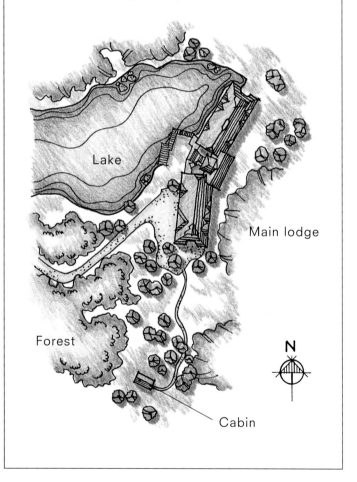

Lake

Main lodge

Forest

N

Cabin

or open to the view. The outdoors comes inside the cabin through a series of French doors, shaped like a half octagon, behind the central fireplace. The high ratio of glass to space was deliberate, to make sure the cabin was filled with light and provided ample views of nature—especially the spectacular variety of wildlife that inhabits a major preserve next to the estate.

"Though it looks like a traditional building, its attitude is modern," says Mark. "The woodwork is very playful, and the cabin is filled with abstract gestures, like the front, which is asymmetrical. The building is meant to be a work of art."

The boardwalk that leads from the main lodge to the Marsh Pavilion invites visitors to enter the cabin up a wide stairway. Mark deliberately set the doorway to the left to signal that, despite its traditional look, this is a modern building. In keeping with the traditional but modern theme, Mark designed an asymmetrical pattern of logs to hold up the porch roof.

Inside, the focal point is the fireplace, with a log mantel and copper facing, which radiates heat into the room and hides a stainless-steel flue. The mantel was constructed from several tree trunks found in an apple orchard in Upstate New York.

BUILT HIGH ABOVE THE FLOODPLAIN, THE CABIN RESTS ON TALL WOODEN POSTS driven 30 ft. to 60 ft. into the marsh. The owners wanted the cabin to function as both indoor and outdoor space so the one-room pavilion is flanked by porches on either end. The wood-shingle roof and the chimney match those of the main lodge.

A BOARDWALK LEADS TO THE CABIN, where a wide stairway invites visitors to enter. Mark set the door to the left to signal that, despite its traditional look, this is a modern building.

IN TUNE WITH THE ENVIRONMENT

The main challenge when building the Marsh Pavilion was safeguarding the ecologically sensitive site from construction damage. That's why Centerbrook architect Mark Simon elected to have as much of the cabin built offsite as possible. A subcontractor, experienced at working with logs, was hired to prefabricate the cabin in his New Jersey workshop according to Mark's drawings.

"We looked into building the cabin with logs that still had the bark, but we discovered that beetles get in there and the bark eventually rots off, so we decided against it," notes Mark.

To give the cabin a secure base, 12 hefty wooden posts were driven deep into the marshy land. A wooden frame platform was then bolted to the posts, and the walls were made with pressure-treated logs that were "fit together like Lincoln Logs," says project manager Doug Winger. Before the two pieces of the gable roof were added, a prefabricated, zero-clearance metal fireplace was positioned inside the cabin.

"Each horizontal log dries and shrinks across its diameter about an inch over the first decade or so," says Mark. "In a couple of years we'll need to jack up the walls and fill them in with an additional log."

A SMALL OUTPOST

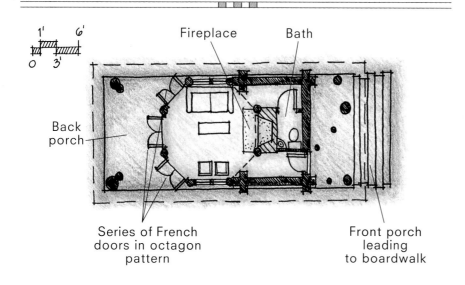

Fireplace

Bath

Back porch

1'   6'

0   3'

Series of French doors in octagon pattern

Front porch leading to boardwalk

THE FOCAL POINT OF THE INTERIOR IS THE FIREPLACE, with its copper facing and log mantel. The copper, which radiates heat into the room and hides the stainless-steel flue, will acquire a rich finish as it ages. The mantel was constructed from several tree trunks found in an apple orchard in Upstate New York. A series of French doors in front of the fireplace flood the interior with light while showing off the marsh outside.

An Interim Strategy

O NE OF THE FIRST THINGS that's needed before creating a retreat is a plot of special land. Often, buying the land taxes a family's resources, which can delay construction. A common strategy for more immediate use of the land is to reduce construction costs and first build a guest cabin, carriage house, or habitable boathouse.

That's the strategy that Ann and Tom Chapman adopted after consulting with architect Robert W. Knight in Blue Hill, Maine. For several years, Knight had been promoting cabin designs in his book *Lucia's Little Houses,* in addition to compiling quite a portfolio of modest structures designed especially for the Maine coast and countryside. So Knight was prepared when the Chapmans spoke of their enchantment with a boathouse they'd seen on the cove and proposed a few possibilities.

First, they wouldn't use the place much, and after a period of some years, they could sell both the land and the boathouse. Second, they would use the land frequently, but only in the summer, so the boathouse would not need insulation or heat. When they retired, they could build a regular summer house. As a third possibility, they

SLEEPING IN THE LOFT IS LIKE LIVING IN AN UNFINISHED ATTIC. No effort was made to hide wiring or framing.

A SLEEPING LOFT OPENS UP OVER THE PORCH. A skylight floods the space with natural sunlight filtered through summer trees. Additional lighting comes from low-voltage spotlights tracked above the beams where electric lines are concealed.

TO COMPLEMENT THE OPEN NATURE OF THE CABIN—with its framing exposed and treated as decorative trim—the small kitchen shows all its contents as well with the use of open shelving.

would use the land frequently, both summer and winter. They could build a larger retirement structure, finishing the boathouse for use as guest facilities and/or office studio. Finally, they would use the land throughout the year but retire elsewhere. Then they could winterize and expand into the boat storage area, keeping the boat elsewhere.

Ann and Tom chose to create a small boathouse with an unfinished interior. Because there was a high probability that the boathouse might not be further improved, special care was taken in its construction. Knight designed shallow rafters, which were placed every 2 ft. and braced with a single collar tie at every other rafter set. The wood was treated more like trim than like framing, and so special care was taken in fastening. Lumber-grade stamps were sanded off, and the roof was sheathed in pine boards instead of plywood for a more pleasing appearance inside. The 6 in. of insulation added on top of the pine sheathing, along with insulated roof windows, ensured that the cabin could be used in the winter.

Although the space is relatively unadorned, it has a special character—casual yet warm, charming, and inviting for most of the year. From the sanctuary of their boathouse, Ann and Tom can contemplate their long-term strategies for the site.

THE OPEN, UNFINISHED CHARACTER OF THE INTERIOR allows the warm tone of the pine to become a design theme. Open kitchen shelving is both an economical measure and a decorative element, as is the plywood and painted floor. A simple Franklin stove helps take away the chill on a wet fall day.

DOWN TOWARD THE COAST

In areas of coastal Maine, like this one near Acadia National Park, it's hard to drive anywhere without having a sense of the sea's nearness. When the car climbs the hill and the ocean comes into view, it's easy to understand why so many people choose to build their cabin on the Maine coast.

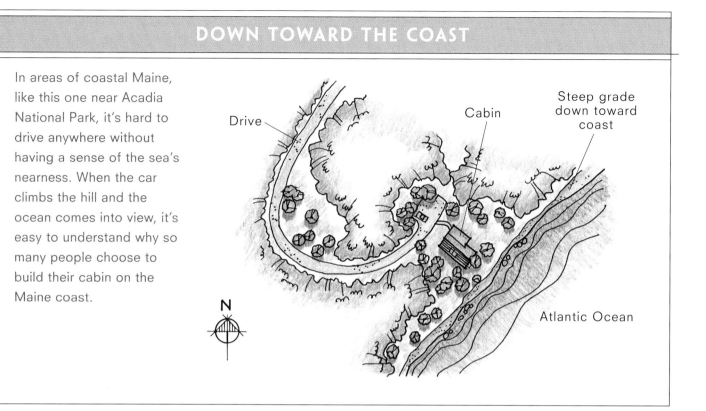

Drive

Cabin

Steep grade down toward coast

N

Atlantic Ocean

THE BUSINESS OF CABINS

Architects design cabins for a variety of reasons: as loss leaders for more lucrative commercial or institutional clients, as experimental testing grounds for themselves as clients, or as gifts for parents. Only a few architects aggressively seek cabin designs as a principal component of their business.

One such architect is Robert W. Knight, whose book *Lucia's Little Houses* is a portfolio of small house designs. From a base in Blue Hill, Maine, he recognizes the importance of this form both for the vacation market and for personal satisfaction.

THIS CABIN IS SITED TO MAXIMIZE the stunning view of the Atlantic Ocean and the Maine coastline. Because of ample light from windows and skylights, the French doors that open onto the porch seem to almost turn the cabin inside out.

OLD-STYLE BARN DOORS ALLOW ACCESS TO THE BOAT below the living area. The balcony above provides space for outdoor living on warm summer days. The cabin's gabled roof and shingled exterior are right at home on the Maine coast. At Tom and Ann Chapman's request, architect Bob Knight kept the forest as close as possible to the boathouse.

SHARING SPACE WITH A BOAT

FIRST FLOOR

Living area
Bedroom
Porch
Stove
Kitchen area
Bath
Entry porch

1'   6'
0   3'

SECOND FLOOR

Skylight
Loft
Loft

the Modern Cabin

SOME RISK TAKERS HAVE FORGED new definitions for places of retreat. By exploring new means of construction, new materials, and new ways of perceiving space, we create the modern cabin. However, sometimes mere whimsy and wonder drive the imagination. Concerns about resale and return on investment are set aside for the sheer joy of fresh, colorful places.

Rocky Mountain Retreat

The fast-moving water and frequent rapids of the Arkansas River, which cascades south through the Rocky Mountains, have attracted many kayakers, including Denver architect Ron Mason. By 1973, he had traversed the river so often that he decided to buy 17 acres of land along its banks near Granite, Colorado. From the site he can also see several 14,000-ft. peaks, including Mounts Harvard and Belford.

Ron didn't begin building until 1983; at first he just camped on his property in a teepee. Then he designed an 18-ft. by 48-ft. log cabin that contains a kitchen, living area, bath, bedroom, and studio loft. That was followed by construction of an 18-ft. by 24-ft. log guest cabin that contains a bedroom and sauna. The two structures are joined by a deck platform, open to the southern sun, with views of the river only yards away and of the distant peaks.

The gold mining history of the area inspired Ron to build with logs, but he used them in a design with a contemporary sense of light and view. The end gables are window walls, French doors lead out to the deck, and skylights punctuate the galvanized metal roof, which

THE OVERLOOK TOWER IS AN ARCHITECTURAL FOLLY. A delight to build, it's used for viewing hawks and eagles. It adds a vertical dimension to Ron Mason's enclave, which also contains two log structures. When the tower is lit up at night, light glows through its lattice-like skin, making the coyotes howl.

RON MASON'S COMPLEX IS ADJACENT TO THE ARKANSAS RIVER, one of North America's premier kayaking routes. After 40 years of kayaking the world's waters, Ron can now step into his hull only a few yards from his cabin, which is connected to a guest cabin by a series of decks.

IN THE LOFT, WITH A KAYAK EVER AT THE READY HANGING OVERHEAD, the gable-end wall of windows affords yet another spectacular view of the rugged Colorado landscape.

RON PURPOSEFULLY CHOSE FURNISHINGS with simple shapes and boldly colored organic fabrics and patterns to extend the cabin's black-and-white theme.

seems to float on the dense log mass. The gabled windows align with the exterior of the logs, whereas the French doors sit inside the log walls. This construction technique provides protection from the elements in a climate with swiftly changing weather.

The most recent construction, an overlook tower, has a metal superstructure clad in pine boards. Boards are spaced $\frac{5}{8}$ in. apart so that when the tower is lit at night from the inside, the walls appear transparent. At the top is a glass cube for observation and starlight sleeping. "From here I can wake up with Mount Belford between my toes," exclaims Ron.

A WARM 15-FT. BY 18-FT., SOUTH-FACING DECK extends living spaces out of doors and connects the main cabin and guest cabin. The project won a Merit Award from *Sunset* magazine in 1995.

AN ARCHITECT'S COMPOUND

With the Colorado Rockies in the background and the rapid Arkansas River right outside the front door, the location of this string of small buildings almost begs people to be outside. Although views throughout the complex are stunning, nothing quite compares to those from the top of the tower.

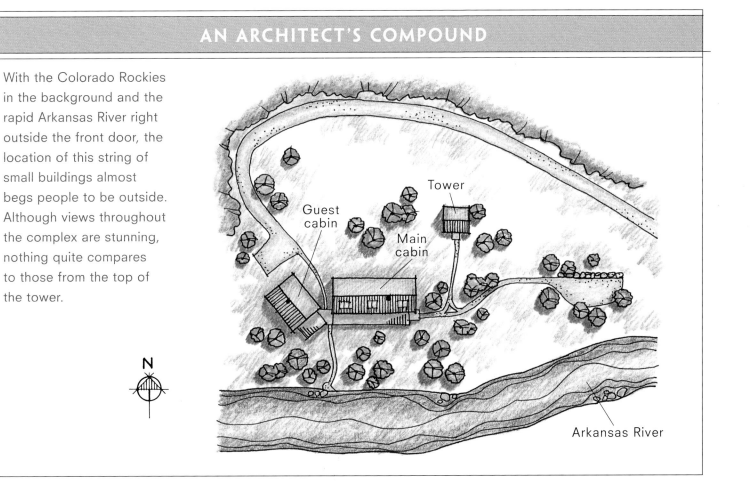

N

Guest cabin

Tower

Main cabin

Arkansas River

AN OPEN PLAN

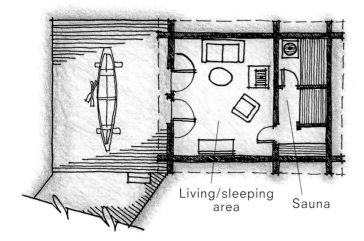

Living/sleeping area

Sauna

MAIN CABIN

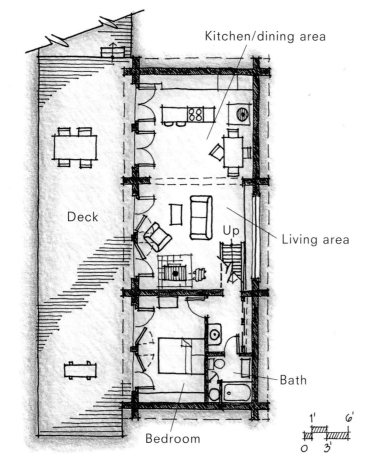

Kitchen/dining area

Deck

Up

Living area

Bath

Bedroom

1'   6'

0   3'

THE CABIN BROKEN APART

Take a house, blow it apart into individual functions, and you get the effect that architect Ron Mason achieved with his personal cabin complex. The main cabin and guest cabin are strewn across one bank of the Arkansas River, separating activity areas that otherwise

THE OVERALL IMPRESSION IS OF A SMALL CAMPUS, WITH BELL TOWER AND LECTURE HALL.

might be found under one roof. Apart from these functional structures is the tower, or folly, that's good only for enjoyment and the occasional overnight campout. The overall impression is of a small campus, with bell tower and lecture hall.

THE INTERIOR SPACE IS AN OPEN PLAN. The warm pine logs contrast with a black metal wood stove and metal stairs to the loft. The floor is southern yellow pine, and the kitchen cabinets are white pine.

Fresh Take on the Log Cabin

CALIFORNIA ARCHITECT THOMAS BLUROCK earns his living building huge public schools in inner cities, so when it came to designing a fishing cabin for himself on a patch of land above Montana's Yellowstone River, he went small, 850 sq. ft. small.

"I've always been fascinated with little living spaces and modesty," he says. "I have this thing about not using more than you need. In southern California, you're in the middle of people who are just outrageously excessive all the time. It drives me wild."

Tom packed a lot into his tiny space with a unique blend of old and new, familiar and unconventional. He chose a classic form—the New England saltbox—but elected to build it with square logs stacked with a traditional Swedish dovetail joint, rather than standard saltbox clapboard siding. He really shook up the formula by opening up the cabin with a 10-ft. by 12-ft. window on the front, faced by a 6½-ft. by 12-ft. sliding door on the back, which gives the 32-ft. by 18-ft. living area (with a 16-ft. ceiling) a sense of see-through spaciousness and a grandeur usually associated with lodges.

ARCHITECT THOMAS BLUROCK HAD THE LARGE FRONT DOOR custom built so it opens top and bottom. He was more concerned about making all the parts of the cabin functional than about making them conventional.

THE WARMTH OF THE CABIN'S INTERIOR radiates outside at night, lighting up the area like a blazing bonfire. Though Tom originally wanted to site the cabin right beside the Yellowstone River, he selected a higher spot so the hills could provide needed protection from the winds.

In keeping with his desire to find "nice ways of doing small stuff," Tom opted for several well-designed European pieces—a compact, see-through German kitchen unit, a cleanly shaped Danish woodstove, and low-voltage Italian lights strung unobtrusively beneath the rafters. A library ladder leads to the loft, eliminating the need for bulky, space-consuming stairs.

"They're all decent functional responses to small spaces," says Tom. "I sort of buy the whole modernist architectural ethic that if you approach something on the basis of quality and just general soundness, and make it do something logically and rationally, the aesthetics will follow."

A PLAYFUL SCALE

Nothing is the right size," Tom Blurock says about his cabin. Least of all the oversize front window that's the cabin's centerpiece. Or the large door directly opposite it. Other windows are low in the kitchen, bedroom, and bathroom and very high in the gable ends. Then there's the custom-made Dutch-style front door that's lower and wider than usual; the contrast between the window and the door is startling.

There's nothing gimmicky or capricious about these design decisions. They allow light to flood the cabin throughout the day, making the interior seem larger than it is, and they focus attention on the land around it.

Inspiration came from a number of sources: a 400-sq.-ft. box that a friend of his father's built in Washington's San Juan Islands; the early houses of Charles Moore, one of the architects of the legendary Sea Ranch on the northern California coast; and the work of San Francisco architect Bernard Maybeck, whose work is known for quirky uses of scale.

"IT'S NOT A KITCHEN; IT'S A PIECE OF FURNITURE," says Tom, who first spotted the space-saving stainless steel kitchen unit in London years ago and filed away the name of the German manufacturer. The attractively designed module, which Tom was able to track down and buy in Los Angeles, includes stove, sink, counterspace, and hanging storage—all in one efficient unit.

TOM SITED HIS CABIN FACING NORTH WITH AN EXPANSIVE VIEW of Paradise Valley, near the entrance to Yellowstone National Park. A line created by that view goes right through the front window. To protect the 6½-ft. by 12-ft. back door from bull elk in rut sparring with their own images in the glass, Tom installed sliding barn doors, which he closes when he's not there.

SITE OFFERS PROTECTION

Practically any vista in the Yellowstone River Valley is beautiful. But finding a site with the ideal balance between a breathtaking view and protection from the rugged Montana elements was essential to the architect–owner.

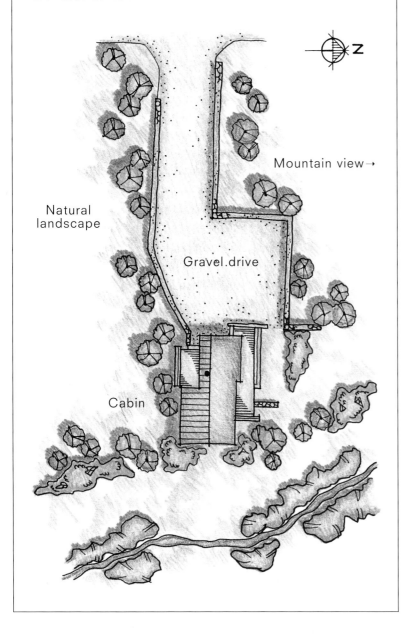

Mountain view→

Natural landscape

Gravel.drive

Cabin

"EVERYTHING WILL GO BACK TO THE LAND, to various shades of gray," says Tom. "Ultimately, nature will take care of the blend."

THE HIGH, OPEN SPACE filled with huge expanses of light from windows both front and back and in the gable ends creates what Tom calls "a National Park–lodge scale" that totally defies the cabin's size.

SEE-THROUGH SPACIOUSNESS

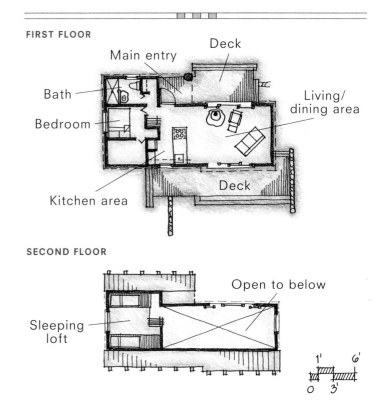

FIRST FLOOR

Main entry

Deck

Bath

Living/ dining area

Bedroom

Kitchen area

Deck

SECOND FLOOR

Open to below

Sleeping loft

Just for the Fun of It

FOLLIES—FANCIFUL OR WHIMSICAL STRUC-
TURES whose sole purpose is to amuse—have
a great tradition in the English landscape. The
Duke of Bedford built a Swiss-style cottage at
Endsleigh in 1815 just so he could look at it high on the
ridge when he was at his hunting lodge in the valley
below. Architect James Stageberg's "The Whim" had similar beginnings.

Stageberg and his wife, author Susan Allen Toth, created
a retreat for themselves in Wisconsin, high above the Mississippi River where it broadens into Lake Pepin. Susan,
who has written about English gardens in several books,
cultivated a colorful landscape in the native Midwestern
forest. James designed an array of colorful, imaginative
buildings: a cottage, a writer's retreat, a storage shed, a
garage, and a garden trellis. One last building was needed
to fill the view amid daffodils and hollyhocks.

The colorful folly James imagined began as his studio
but evolved into a guest cabin even before it was built. He
wanted something vertical and thus the 13-ft.-high multi-
purpose form takes its cues from the curves in the earlier
buildings in the compound and from the teepee that once

**ONE OF THE MOST ORIGINAL FEATURES OF "THE WHIM"
IS THE CEILING,** with its red dot centered on green
slats that cover joints of maple plywood.

ARCHITECT JAMES STAGEBERG'S BRIGHT PURPLE SILO,
with contrasting magenta trim, sits at one end
of a flower garden next to a Wisconsin forest.
Originally designed as an open structure, the
tapered tower evolved from a mere architectural
folly into a cozy guest cabin. Many of the buildings in the Stageberg compound explore similar
possibilities of round shapes.

CURLY MAPLE CABINETS WITH EXPOSED DOVETAILS SHOW THE HIGH LEVEL OF WORKMANSHIP that went into the cabin. Because major cooking isn't required, a refrigerator, microwave oven, and coffeepot are the extent of the minimal kitchen.

SITTING LIKE A GARDEN ORNAMENT

Sitting in the middle of flower gardens with views to the forest and the nearby Mississippi River, the 13-ft.-tall cabin is so sculptural that it serves not only as a guest cabin but also as a large garden ornament. Sharing the garden with the cabin are a garden house, writer's retreat, storage shed, garage, and trellis.

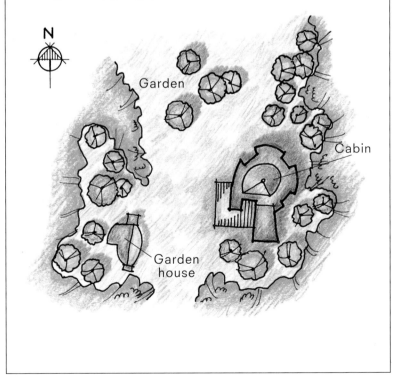

stood nearby. James attached a bathroom shed for a grand total of 210 sq. ft. Carpenter John May built the tapering tower "as if it were a fine piece of furniture," notes Susan. Calling it "The Whim" was an apt afterthought.

Not only is the guest cabin fun to look at from the outside, it's pleasing from within. Lying in bed, one can look up at the "Eye of God" ceiling, its red dot centered on green staves. Lantern windows of art glass flood light across the ceiling, while simple double-hung windows offer views of the colorful flower gardens and the forest beyond. James's beautifully crafted Whim, with its careful sense of gaiety, won a 1997 AIA Minnesota design award. To learn more about the compound, called "Wind Whistle," read *A House of One's Own* by James Stageberg and Susan Allen Toth (Clarkson Potter, 1991).

A WHIMSICAL SILO

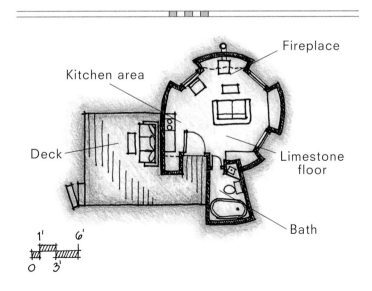

BRIGHTLY COLORED FURNITURE, WHICH MATCH THE PAINTED CEILING, the exterior, and
the nearby flower garden, fills the interior living/sleeping space with cheer. A woodstove, artfully positioned between two windows, warms the space in cool weather.

Academic Freedom

Parents have often been early patrons in a young architect's emerging career. Mike and Penny Winton selected architect Frank Gehry for their guest house in the Minneapolis suburbs, but turned to son Nick and his friend Catherine Veikos when they needed a guest cabin adjacent to their 65-year-old log house on the north shore of Lake Superior. Although they were still students of architecture, Nick and Catherine were up to the challenge of creating a design for the elder Wintons.

Nick and Catherine's design stayed true to the log character of the adjacent house by using more than 100 white pine logs ranging in size from 9 in. to 14 in. in diameter. They developed a linear scheme that's banked into the side of the hill overlooking the lake. Access to the cabin is from either side on the lower level where kitchen, bath, and living space can be found. Sleeping on this level is on built-in benches beyond the see-through fireplace. An open stair provides access to the upper level where guests can sleep in the prow or in the two bedrooms at the rear.

LOGWORK USUALLY INVOLVES SIMPLE RECTANGLES. Here, however, the logs meet at unusual angles, which required great care when fitting them tightly together.

THE CENTRAL FIREPLACE IS TWO SIDED and rises to the top of the 18-ft.-high central sitting room. It is sheathed in earth-toned tiles created by ceramic artist Connie Mayron. The color of the tiles ties in with the spectacular stone boulders that dot the North Shore landscape. A warm fir floor adds a touch of red against the white pine logs.

SETTING A COURSE FOR OPEN WATER

Pointing toward the lake like the prow of a dry-docked ship, the log cabin is built into a hill that descends toward Lake Superior. Here, 250 years ago, fur traders in birch-bark canoes and wooden bateaux crisscrossed the lake; later, Mackinaw boats, schooners, steamers, and iron-ore freighters traveled the waters.

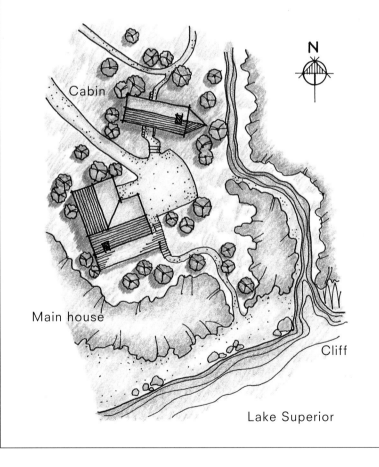

Log construction has a particular discipline. Logs need corners to stabilize the walls, whose length is limited by the length of the logs. The logs in the prow are tied together at the base below the corner windows and are tied above with the metal frame of the children's sleeping loft. Nick notes that "this is certainly not a radical design, but it is perhaps a little experimental." He credits his parents with giving him the freedom to explore ideas and the responsibility to make a few mistakes.

He extols the virtues also of builder Richard Stone for heading a skilled crew that accomplished this task during a cold Minnesota winter. As to the logs, Nick says, "They have a life of their own that you just can't imagine when you're drawing. They are very beautiful, almost sensual."

ONE OF THE ARCHTECTS' PLAYFUL TOUCHES was to extend the logs from the cabin to the entryway outside. A path connects the guest cabin to the main house.

THE WINDOWS IN THE PROW RISE UP FROM THE FIRST TO THE SECOND FLOOR. At night, these windows project like a beacon into the night air.

INSIDE THE PROW DOWNSTAIRS, a window seat wraps around the sharp angle of the room to form an extra couple of beds for guests or children. Built-in storage beneath makes clever use of what would otherwise be wasted space.

A SEAT ON LAKE SUPERIOR

A prow such as this is unique in log construction, which usually dictates that windows can be no closer than about 4 ft. to a corner. Serving as a column, corners hold the whole together providing the strength of the log structure. The logs in this prow are thus held together by mechanical means.

What's unique here is that the logic of the log construction method is challenged to offer new design opportunities. The prow is not just a prow; it's a prow with a window in it. The space in the prow is narrow and promotes the notion of a person sitting alone, projected out into the exterior world—in this case, the world of Lake Superior.

JUST INSIDE THE BACK DOOR, cleverly positioned pine dowels set into and between wooden posts hold tiny pegs for hanging coats, hats, and mittens. Dowels that don't contain pegs simply act as decorative accents, creating an interesting contrast with the thick logs of the wall.

AN INTERIOR CROSS WALL, which wouldn't exist in a traditional log cabin, is cut off to create an opening for the kitchen and bath behind the main living area. The butts provide rustic texture that contrasts with the modern kitchen.

LIKE A SHIP

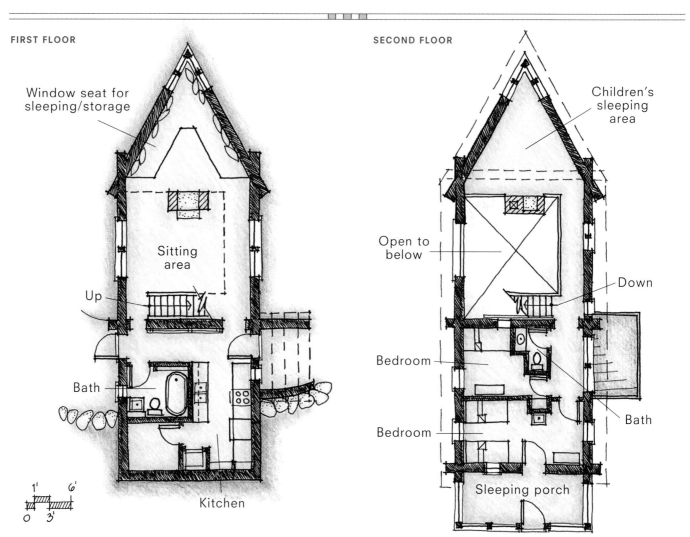

FIRST FLOOR

Window seat for sleeping/storage

Sitting area

Up

Bath

Kitchen

SECOND FLOOR

Children's sleeping area

Open to below

Down

Bedroom

Bedroom

Bath

Sleeping porch

Contemporary Dogtrot

FOR MORE THAN 20 YEARS, as their kids were growing up, John and Brenda Atkinson would take the 20-minute drive from their home in Baton Rouge, Louisiana, to escape the city heat and enjoy their old cabin and swimming pool on a few acres of land north of town. Then, for more than a decade, the Atkinsons let the property lapse while they and their children got away to a nearby lake where they kept a boat.

But once their children were grown, the couple decided to return to this peaceful and more private rural setting. Their son, Stephen, by now an architect in Boston, was called back to design a retreat for a priest friend of the family. When the priest changed his plans, John and Brenda asked their son to build the retreat for them instead.

Stephen decided that what would be appropriate for the few acres of land was a cabin that paid homage to the historic Southern dogtrot. Traditionally, a dogtrot is two buildings or two halves of a building that are separated by an open breezeway covered by an extended gable roof. The breezeway, or open center hall, allows air circulation

SIDE WINDOWS ARE GLAZED OUTSIDE with corrugated translucent siding. Inside, the openings are glazed in translucent plastic for continuity with the wall surface. These windows reinforce the ecclesiastical feeling of the space by creating an interior glow akin to stained glass.

A CONTEMPORARY DOGTROT nestles in a thriving grove of pines and hardwoods. The pines, which the Atkinson family planted nearly 10 years ago, provide a private sanctuary for family activities. The family uses the meadow as a ball field.

and provides an outdoor area that's protected from the weather—and, most important, the incessant southern sun.

In Stephen's design, this central space is extended as a deck on the east and west sides, which gives the plan a cruciform design, suggesting the original intention of a priest's house. Depending on the season, outdoor living means either welcoming the sun or hiding from it. Since the eastern deck has an outdoor fireplace and stair access from the driveway, it functions like a central living room, especially during large family gatherings. Of course, the chimney is also reminiscent of the chimney stacks left standing after the destruction of many Southern homes and plantations during the Civil War.

The dogtrot design purposefully separates living and sleeping spaces. The living half contains kitchen, storage, dining, and sitting areas. The bedroom wing includes the bathroom. These separate wings are joined symbolically by four pairs of French doors along the north–south gable axis. Although the cabin has modest sleeping provisions for overnight stays, because it's so near their home in Baton Rouge, the Atkinsons use it primarily during the day. John, for instance, often goes to the cabin to read *The New York Times* and do his daily jog.

THE DECK HAS EAST AND WEST WINGS with a covered central space. The Atkinsons enjoy the walk from the enclosed living area to the sleeping area through the covered breezeway. On cool evenings, a fire in the outdoor fireplace creates a pleasant place to sit and enjoy the outdoors.

A LETTER HOME FROM THE ARCHITECT

Editor's note: Architect Stephen Atkinson wrote a letter to his parents describing the inspiration for his design. The following is excerpted from it.

Family,

This is a copy of the "Zachary house" design. After reading it carefully, you may wish to think of a few more ideas latent in the house.

. . . One could also draw inferences from the cruciform plan shape if they so desired. Just as one enters past the water at St. Aloysius (symbolizing baptism), in this house one enters past the hearth or fire. I found this a fitting and appropriately symbolic way of entering a house versus a chapel. If you think of it, the fire or hearth is the center of a home. It's where the food is prepared, and it's where everyone gathers around for warmth—at least symbolically. Thus it becomes the threshold. Entry onto the deck thus becomes an invitation to change one's mindset.

. . . I very much think every house needs that architectural aspect which holds/represents the spiritual. In the most poetic of ways, this empty spot between the two living units is the heart of the house. It's also the hardest part of the house to explain, even though it's the deepest part—it's beyond me . . .

CATCHING EVERY POSSIBLE BREEZE

In this part of southeastern Louisiana, the summer heat and humidity begin in April and don't slack off until well into October, which makes the capture of every possible breeze important to human comfort. The north–south orientation of the cabin, the east–west breezeway, and the screened double-doors that open onto the breezeway are time-tested Southern methods of getting maximum air circulation.

IMPROVISATION ON A DOGTROT

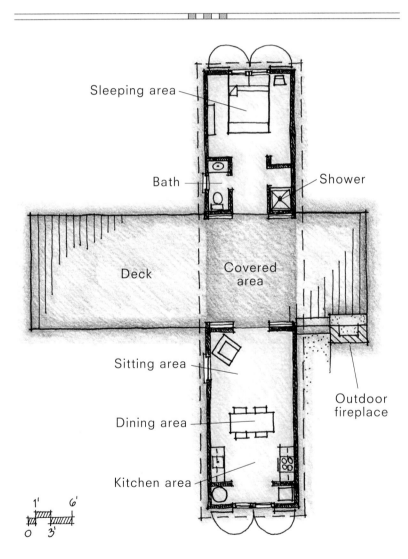

Sleeping area

Bath

Shower

Deck

Covered area

Sitting area

Outdoor fireplace

Dining area

Kitchen area

THE FRENCH DOORS ARE SECURED BY OUTER DOORS, clad in galvanized metal, for protection from weather and vandals. Roll-up screens provide protection from insects and allow ventilation in both wings. Four possibilities exist with each pair of French doors: wide open, screened, glassed for a full view, or closed and secure. The doors swing in, the screens roll up, and the metal doors hinge outward so they can be latched to the walls.

THE POSITION OF THE FIXED DINING TABLE SUGGESTS AN ALTAR, which architect Stephen Atkinson included in his original design for a priest's house. That position also reflects his desire for a spiritual retreat that honors nature.

A Cabin as Ship

Davic and Barbara Yaukey had vacationed with their two sons on Nova Scotia's Blanche Peninsula for a decade before buying property. Initially fascinated by island living, they found that Eel Bay was more accessible by car. Besides, they liked the southern view over the bay and the protection it provided from northern storms.

While poking around, they discovered an old foundation on their land; it seems a village had once been settled there. Building on land rich in history appealed to them. They selected architect Bryan MacKay-Lyons, known for his interest in regional buildings and local boat-building traditions, to design their cabin.

The Yaukeys had a limited budget so MacKay-Lyons proposed building the cabin in phases. Phase one included the basic structural skin—leaving the building exposed and raw, like a wide-open barn—and essential services such as a bathroom. The Yaukeys were able to live in the shell as though it were a loft and then gradually fill in partition walls, additional storage, details, and site development as their budget allowed.

A WARM MORNING SUN WAKES UP THE SHELTERED DECK. Eel Bay laps at the shore 40 ft. below, as sea gulls and osprey sail by on hunting missions. The exterior material—cedar shingles and pine decking, posts, and trim—were allowed to weather to a rich and natural silver gray.

THE FRAMING IN THE LIVING AREA WAS PREFABRICATED and then quickly assembled at the site in only 2 weeks and without the benefit of electricity. Though originally left exposed to keep costs down, the owners find the raw interior has considerable charm. Now they don't want to change it.

Though the cabin's design is unusual, Barbara appreciates its simplicity. "We are burlap people," she notes, "seeking neither glossy finishes nor hidden mechanics." David likes the openness both inside and out. "Windows make it," he says. "You don't have to search for views." Now the Yaukeys enjoy vacations filled with kayaking and bird watching, made easy from the base of their nautical retreat.

A ZERO-CLEARANCE METAL FIREPLACE IS EXPOSED through decorative wood cribbing. This lightweight design can easily rest on normal wood framing and needs no masonry support. A noncombustible hearth is inlaid into the floor.

KITCHENWARE IS STORED IN OPEN SHELVING, allowing both fine pottery and simple, utilitarian cookware to function as decoration. The openness of the cabin's storage, which suggests lobster trap construction, lets the lovely coastal light of Nova Scotia flow freely into the cabin.

DESIGNING LIKE A SHIP BUILDER

Architect Brian Mackay-Lyon's work is grounded in the maritime and agrarian culture of Nova Scotia. As a young boy he watched the boat-building process and was fascinated as a large steam chest was used to contour wood into desired shapes. Although he recognizes that his buildings are not boats, he enjoys the workability and lightness of wood and uses it liberally to give his structures form.

The Yaukey site was off grid, which required the prefabrication of many structural components elsewhere. But working with prefabricated parts made for quick assembly—it took just 14 days to put the whole cabin together. Curved, laminated posts and beams share structural duty with standard stud framing—all

wrapped in a tight skin of wood shingles. Metal was used sparingly as framing brackets, stair stringers, balcony pipe rails, and for the fireplace. Windows and skylights were introduced with discretion. The larger skylights open up to views of the bay, and the smaller ones allow the sun to brighten an otherwise dark corner. Like the efficiency of old wooden rowboat construction, the Mackay-Lyon's design gains its elegance from minimalism and utility.

CABIN WITH A SLANT

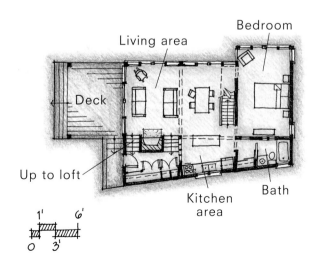

Living area

Bedroom

Deck

Up to loft

Kitchen area

Bath

1' 6'

0   3'

A BIG BARN FEELING—PLENTY OF OPENNESS AND HIGH SPACE—is what the Yaukeys wanted. The curved roof structure is readily visible inside the cabin.

A HIGH VIEW OF EEL BAY

The cabin sits on a high bluff facing westward to Eel Bay, which is on the Blanche Peninsula on the south coast of Nova Scotia, providing memorable views over the water. Several old stone foundations from an earlier settlement dot the site.

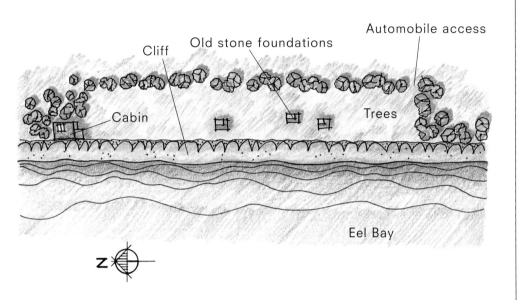

Cliff

Old stone foundations

Automobile access

Cabin

Trees

Eel Bay

Z

THE SPACIOUS DECK IS SHADED in the morning but flooded with sun in the afternoon. This sheltered outdoor room greatly extends the cabin's overall living space.

BECAUSE THE INTERIOR OF THE CABIN IS COMPLETELY OPEN, segregation of function is defined by placement. Here, for instance, a side table and rocking chair, set up in a corner near the front door, are all that's needed to create a reading nook.

In Nature and of Nature

THE EXTERIOR FORM OF THIS CABIN IS LIKE A PRIMITIVE LEAN-TO, with its back to the hillside. A sloping shed roof lifts to the sun, shaded by deciduous trees in summer and open to the warmth of the low sun in winter.

C ABINS AND COTTAGES ARE OFTEN PLACES that nurture us with nature and where nature means natural materials. No American architect explored questions of nature and natural elements in design and construction more than Frank Lloyd Wright. He designed places that sought not to reinterpret nature but rather to be part of it. He sought the potential of living in and of nature, not on or near it. Many of his books, including *The Natural House, The Nature of Materials,* and *Organic Architecture,* reflect that philosophy.

One of Wright's last commissions, conceived in 1957, was the modest Seth Peterson Cottage at Lake Dalton, Wisconsin, now part of Mirror Lake State Park, which rents it out for overnight stays—though there is always a lengthy waiting list. (Unfortunately, neither Wright nor Peterson lived to see construction completed.) On the prow of a hill overlooking the native forest surrounding Mirror Lake, this modest structure exemplifies Wright's lifetime search to create a natural place.

On a plinth of flagstone he centered a gigantic stone hearth in the spirit and character of local stone ledges. He

THE UNFINISHED CABIN SAT VACANT FOR MANY YEARS until a special conservancy restored it. Eifler & Associates ended up reconstructing nearly the entire structure between 1992 and 1993. The roof was rebuilt as well as the floor, a new central heating system was installed, and the cabin was totally rewired.

BUILT FROM ITS SITE

On a small hill overlooking Mirror Lake in central Wisconsin sits one of Frank Lloyd Wright's last works, a small cabin built mostly of materials found on the land around it. With its large windows facing the lake and the forest, the cabin provides the least possible barrier between inside and out.

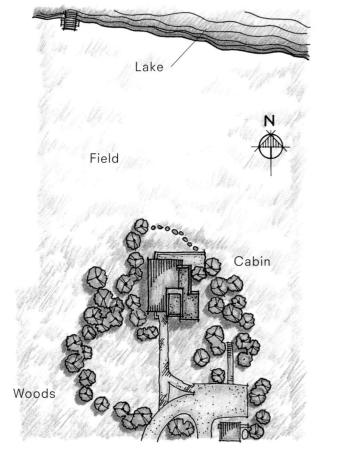

sloped a broad roof to open to the southern sun and designed a window wall that is less about view than about giving the inhabitants the feeling that they're outdoors. The window mullions, or dividers, that Wright designed are like tree trunks, and the diagonal members above are like branches and leaves. Even the stones in the bathroom create the feeling of standing in a grotto waterfall, not a manufactured shower enclosure. In the daytime, the light quality outside is the same as that indoors. Shadow patterns are more like those found on a forest floor than on a cabin floor.

Anthropologists have recorded people's primitive attraction to refuge. We seek a natural place of shelter with our back protected from wind and predator, facing the sunshine and the world around us. With the Seth Peterson Cottage design, Frank Lloyd Wright returns us to that place.

SAVING A LOCAL TREASURE

Because the client died before the project was completed, Wright's cabin sat derelict and neglected for several years. In 1988, the building came under the stewardship of the Seth Peterson Cottage Conservancy and was restored under the direction of Eifler & Associates. The cabin was rigorously reconstructed; each floor slab was raised for new heating and wiring. The windows were replaced, and original Wright furniture was reconstructed and refurbished. Today the cabin is available for overnight stays, where guests can enjoy treks in the adjoining Wisconsin nature preserve.

THE CABIN WAS RIGOROUSLY RECONSTRUCTED; EACH FLOOR SLAB WAS RAISED FOR NEW HEATING AND WIRING.

THE CENTRAL MASS OF THE STONE fireplace organizes the utilities of kitchen and bathing. Around this central block, a light, wooden structure defines the living space, including dining, sitting, and sleeping. Above the kitchen and bath is a small storage area. Picture windows open the interior up to the surrounding woodland.

BOTH NATURAL AND MANUFACTURED MATERIALS, such as plywood, went into the cabin. The stone used for the hearth and fireplace is also the flooring material. Wright even extended it outside for a terrace that overlooks the lake.

THE CABIN CONTAINS CLASSIC WRIGHT FURNITURE, some of which was specially constructed. Other pieces were added to complete the project. Characteristic of many Wrightian interiors is the built-in cushioned bench, which serves as principal seating in the living room.

THE WRIGHT FLOOR PLAN

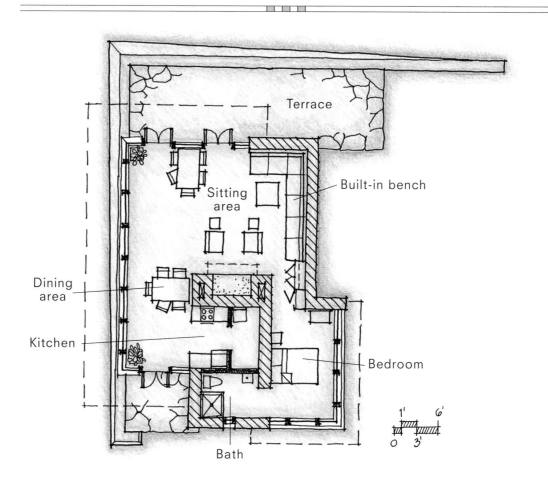

Terrace

Built-in bench

Sitting area

Dining area

Kitchen

Bedroom

Bath

The Call of Loons and Ospreys

TWO YOUNG INTERN ARCHITECTS, Annie Ryan and Bryan Meyer, sought to apply their skills designing a minimalist retreat in the northern Minnesota woods near the Canadian border. Annie and Bryan had camped often on her family's land but wanted a more permanent shelter from rain, cold, and pesky mosquitoes.

They had grown to relish the calls of osprey and loons and, therefore, selected a site fronting on a national forest and Lake Clara where human noises would not intrude on their world. They called their design "The Echo," because of its mute call to the wild in their absence and because the cabin becomes acoustically alive in their presence.

Their budget, environmental concerns, sweat equity, and limited time all suggested a modest structure. The 10-ft. by 24-ft. shed they created is sheathed in economical yet durable cement fiberboard and capped by a corrugated metal roof. The interior is clad in warm yet practical birch-faced plywood; floors are particleboard with a clear finish. A woodstove extends seasonal use beyond just summer. Doors open like flower petals to the lake to the

THIS MINIMALIST CABIN SITS ON ITS LITTLE HILL in the far northern Minnesota woods like an open chest. The owners used to camp on the site, but decided that they needed a basic shelter to protect them from the bugs and weather. The post was set outside to hold the wide window–door open in the wind.

WITH DOORS WIDE OPEN, THE STOVE INSIDE GLOWS brightly as a fire in the pit outside lights the night. When the fire pit burns cold, the insulated doors can be closed to trap in the heat for a good night's sleep.

northwest and the bonfire pit and the forest to the southwest. Cooking takes place outdoors, currently in the fire
pit or the cooking tent, later to be replaced by a cooking
cabin. A guest sleeping cabin is also anticipated. Water
must be transported to the site for cooking and drinking.

A cabin's success can be measured in many ways. Annie
and Bryan began dating during two years of camping at
the site, followed by two years of construction. The cabin's
completion coincided with their marriage there, surrounded by family, loons, and osprey.

**ACCORDION-LIKE, THE SOUTH-
FACING BI-FOLD DOORS OPEN** to let
in a wall of light. To control light
and breezes, the doors can shut
up the cabin drum tight, be
opened one at a time or all partway, or be flung wide open to
expose the interior to everything
the day has to offer.

SHARING NATURE WITH THE BIRDS

In the far northern woods of Minnesota, near Canada, sits a 10-ft. by 24-ft. box of a cabin near a lake. The cabin shelters its owners from the elements and bugs; though when it's time for cooking or bathing, those functions take place outdoors.

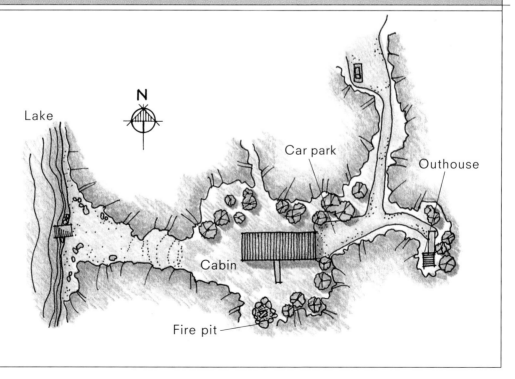

N

Lake

Car park

Outhouse

Cabin

Fire pit

A VERSATILE FOLDING BOX

This cabin has three states: completely corked-up and empty; closed off so it can be warmed during cool nights when people are there; and various levels of openness to induce ventilation, provide a view, and connect to the outside. Here, a number of important functions take place outside the cabin, such as cooking and bathing.

IT DOESN'T PRETEND TO BE ANYTHING MORE THAN BASIC SHELTER.

It would have been easy to add visual baggage to this cabin in the form of gables and dormers, or details like a circular window or hand-crafted door. This cabin makes no such attempt to be fancy. It shelters by its simple skin, shedding the rain away from the opening. It comes alive when people use it. And it doesn't pretend to be anything more than basic shelter.

THE LATTICED WALL PANEL, WHEN NOT SERVING AS A SLEEPING PLATFORM, is hinged to the wall to create an open and spacious interior. When Annie Ryan and Bryan Meyer want to convert the space into a bedroom, the hinged wall panel is folded down. A storage bench is slid under the bottom for additional support. During the day, the foam mattress and bedding are stored in the bench, which serves as a seat or side table when the bed platform is up.

UNFOLDING TO NATURE

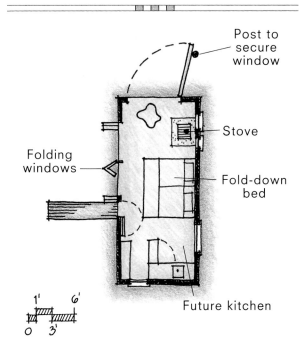

Post to secure window

Stove

Folding windows

Fold-down bed

Future kitchen

1' 6'
0 3'

Floating on a Wisconsin Prairie

A RETURN TO NATURE DRIVES many a cabin design but none more than the Rapsons' glass cube. After Ralph and Mary Rapson purchased an idyllic 40-acre meadow in Wisconsin in 1972, they walked the site as Ralph, a professor of architecture at the University of Minnesota, sketched. But when they studied his early drawings, they noted that walls made of solid materials would block the views. The only solution, they concluded, was all-glass walls. But no one had ever built an all-glass cabin before.

After extensive exploration of that idea, Ralph designed a glass cube containing two floating platforms, or floors, for sitting and sleeping areas. Even the deck on the main level appears to float on a sea of crushed white marble. Only the bathroom is an enclosed space for privacy when bathing and dressing. The solid bathroom form helps define the main floor into kitchen, eating, and sitting areas. A floor hatch in the kitchen provides access to the mechanical space below.

Built in 1974, the design features an ingenious arrangement of Anderson windows and sliding glass doors

THE WALLS ARE REALLY A GROUPING of sliding-glass doors and windows that are stacked, two abreast and three high to form the exterior walls, which are held in place by exterior framing.

RALPH RAPSON'S GLASS CUBE CABIN seems to float on the Wisconsin countryside. Four walls of glass, supported by an exterior structure of posts and braces, holds up the cabin and allows it to flex in the wind.

THE MAIN FLOOR IS DIVIDED INTO KITCHEN, eating, and sitting areas. A floor hatch in the kitchen provides access to the mechanical space below. The detail (left) shows the wood decking resting on a bed of crushed white marble.

A CLEAR VISION

Forty acres of Wisconsin meadowland, a small river down a slight hill, and all the light that the world around can provide are daily fare for the owners of this glass-walled cabin.

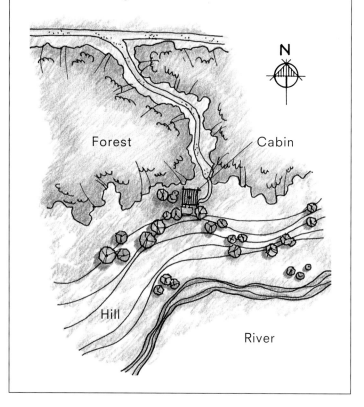

stacked two abreast and three high to form a 26-ft. cube. Living there, with no protection from the elements, has had a strong effect on the Rapsons' daily life. They're awakened by the rich, cool colors of the sunrise and go to sleep with the deeper warmer colors of the sunset. When Ralph sees a storm brewing in the distance, complete with flashes of lightening and booms of thunder, Mary dives for cover in the small mechanical room below ground.

"The good thing about a house like this is that you are a part of nature without being dependent upon it. We can be self-sufficient and enjoy our surroundings without being intrusive," states Ralph.

Besides bringing great pleasure to Ralph and Mary's extended family, the cabin has also become a site for pilgrimages by architectural students from around the world. The cabin has won several awards, including a 25-year award from the Minnesota Society of Architects.

CLEAR STRENGTH

The elegance of the Rapson cabin comes from the minimalization of the structure. Windows are not set into a wall; they are the wall. Their frame is made rigid by extension to an external structure that supports the bracing, which allows the cabin to flex in a strong Wisconsin wind.

The frame is a combination of four 12-ft. squares with 4-in. by 4-in. wood posts at their corners, along with a special 6-in. by 6-in. cut-wood post at the center. Beams, 2 in. by 12 in. and 4 in. by 12 in., connect across the space 7 ft. above base level and again at the roof. The upper sleeping platform is hung from the roof structure by ½-in. rods and a dozen anchor brackets. These horizontal frames extend outward 4 ft. beyond the window wall to anchored 4-in. by 4-in. posts at the perimeter. On this perimeter frame, each 12-ft. section is wind-braced with diagonal ½-in. tie rods with adjustable turnbuckles.

The perimeter columns are thus 4 ft. in from the perceived corner of the structure, creating a light openness at the corners. The whole frame, along with tie rods, is painted black, giving the illusion of steel while also appearing to recede. The frames of the glass are white. Collectively, the white-on-black structure forms a pattern that borders views through the cabin and beyond.

THE SPIRAL STAIRCASE LEADS FROM THE MAIN TO THE SECOND FLOOR, and a ship's ladder (top right, upstairs) provides access to the top sleeping loft. Banners, wind socks, kites, and flags often hang from the ceiling, providing a colorful floating environment like an Alexander Calder mobile.

TRANSPARENT CUBE

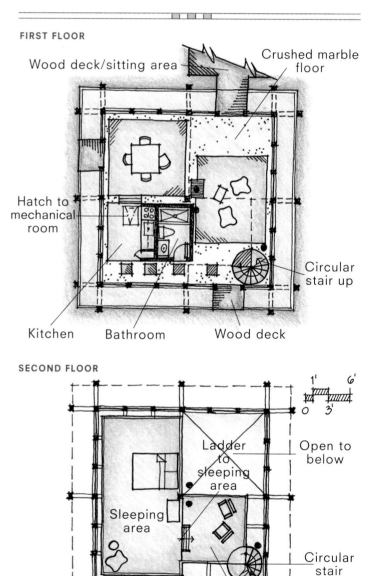

FIRST FLOOR

Wood deck/sitting area

Crushed marble floor

Hatch to mechanical room

Kitchen   Bathroom   Wood deck

Circular stair up

SECOND FLOOR

Ladder to sleeping area

Open to below

Sleeping area

Circular stair

Intermediate deck

THE CABIN SITS ATOP A RIVER EMBANKMENT in the rolling Wisconsin countryside. A pine grove was planted to the north and west to shelter the cube from northern winds and to provide privacy from the road. The upstairs sleeping area offers a view to the small river that winds off into the distance.

A Salute to Frank Lloyd Wright

KEVIN GORDON'S CABIN ON FLATHEAD LAKE isn't called "Duck Shack" because it's a duck shack. It's the name Kevin's dad, Jack, gave the rustic cabin he built there for duck hunting in the mid-1960s. About 30 years later, after the old place was overrun by mice and bugs, Kevin, a trained architect who runs the Missoula, Montana, construction company his grandfather started in 1934, decided it was time to build a new cabin.

The first thing Kevin did was find a new site, which he discovered one day while fixing the roof of the old outhouse. The view of the skeet field and the lake from that outhouse roof was spectacular, which led him to think of the new place as a sort of lookout tower, a familiar sight in the Montana wilderness. The most powerful influence on his tower design came from Frank Lloyd Wright, whose work Kevin had admired since his teens when an aunt who lived in Wright's hometown sent him a scrapbook about Wright's career. Discovering that the Pella Window Company produced Wright-inspired Prairie-style windows, Kevin decided to design a two-story structure with walls of windows encircling the upper floor.

ALTHOUGH THE EXTERIOR WAS INITIALLY MODELED AFTER a Montana fire lookout tower, Kevin Gordon's major inspiration was Frank Lloyd Wright, whose influence is seen in the arched door, ribbon of Prairie-style windows enclosing the upper floor, long roof overhang, and dramatically cantilevered deck.

THE SITTING AREA, WHICH WAS PLACED IN THE CORNER to get natural light on two sides, contains just a few simple pieces of furniture. For instance, the far chair was designed by Gustav Stickley, a contemporary of Wright who emphasized natural materials in his Arts and Crafts style designs.

All that glass posed problems, however. How do you tie the roof securely to the walls and hold the second floor steady in the wind with all that glass? Steel. Kevin installed steel columns at the four corners and tied them to a tension ring in the roof. The steel stiffens the walls and secures the roof. Cantilevering the deck was also tricky, but again steel was the answer. Kevin installed a large steel column ("as big as a car") in the center of the first floor of the building and attached to it three steel beams that radiate out and form the support for the deck, which can hold up to 87 people.

Now used for skeet shooting, clay shooting, and annual Fourth of July gatherings of friends from around the West, the Duck Shack won the 1996 Honor Award from Montana's chapter of the American Institute of Architects. The jury said the design "is a very strong concept, beautifully and consistently detailed."

"THE PELLA WINDOW COMPANY started making what they call Prairie-style windows a few years ago," notes Kevin. "They have a Frank Lloyd Wright feel, and I decided they fit in with the character of what I wanted to do." Although they open out, the ample overhang on the house protects the windows from weather.

AT FIRST, KEVIN COULDN'T FIGURE OUT HOW TO CREATE RAILING FOR THE DECK that wouldn't also block the view. When the metal posts were installed, he remembered the rope life lines that encircle his sailboat. So with eye rings welded to the posts, he strung sailboat line between them in an ingenious criss-cross design, achieving the right effect.

THE OWNER CHOSE BLACK MARBLE FOR THE KITCHEN COUNTERTOPS to complement the cherry cabinets, floors, and woodwork. The stove, refrigerator, and sink are built along one wall, with storage in the adjoining island.

LOOKING OUT ON THE WORLD

Flathead Lake, the largest freshwater lake west of the Mississippi River, looms large in maps of northwestern Montana. For the cabin to take in views of the lake from where it sat, it would have to rise up from the ground. Thanks to its towering form, this two-story cabin commands a spectacular view of the lake to the west and of the rugged Montana wilderness all around.

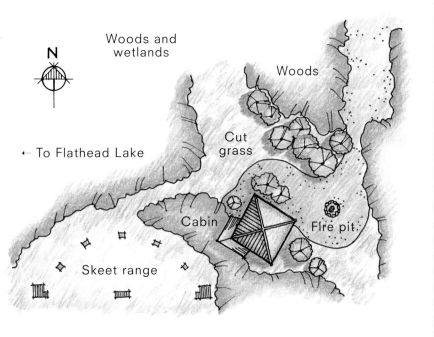

Woods and wetlands

N

Woods

← To Flathead Lake

Cut grass

Cabin

Fire pit

Skeet range

AN ECHO OF THE EARLY PRAIRIE SCHOOL

The style is early Wright, or early Chicago Prairie School, just after the turn of the last century. The young architect was moving from a European influence to search for an American architecture. As he looked to the West, Wright saw the prairie and its horizontal lines. The older European lines were vertical, looking skyward from their dense cities. Wright concentrated on the horizontal.

THIS CABIN IS A DIRECT DESCENDANT OF FRANK LLOYD WRIGHT.

The roof became a hat and the base became an extension of the earth, with the masonry thrusting up toward the roof. Windows fit into a horizontal zone that's offset by strong vertical lines. This cabin is a direct descendant of Frank Lloyd Wright, down to the arched portal, which echoes a house Wright designed in Oak Park, Illinois, where he first established his name.

KEVIN ARTFULLY TUCKED THE STAIRS that lead to the ground floor (which houses the bathroom and garage) behind the kitchen area.

ATOP A TOWER

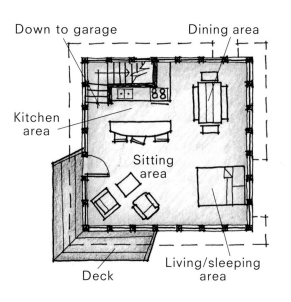

Down to garage

Dining area

Kitchen area

Sitting area

Living/sleeping area

Deck

THE 24-FT. BY 24-FT. ONE-ROOM CABIN HAS FOUR DISTINCT AREAS: dining, kitchen and bar, sitting, and sleeping. Yet because of the abundance of light and the high peaked ceiling, the room seems spacious. Kevin chose to keep it uncluttered so that the focus would be on the "beauty of the building" and not on what's in it.

Credits

half-title page: Photo © davidduncanlivingston.com.; frontispiece: Photo © Randy O'Rourke; p. v: Photo © John Anthony Rizzo; p. vi (top left): Photo © Charles Register; p. vi (top right, bottom left): Photo © davidduncanlivingston.com; p. vi (bottom right): Photo © Chipper Hatter; p. 1: Photo © Rob Karosis.

Introduction
p. 2 (left): Photo © Rob Karosis; pp. 2 (right) and 3: Photos © davidduncanlivingston.com.

For the Love of Cabins
pp. 4, 6, 8 (right), 10, 11, 16 (top), and 20 (bottom): Photos © Dale Mulfinger; p. 5: Photo © Jerry Whaley; p. 7: Photo © Sheila Hunt, A.I.A, Architect and Terry McGee, Artist; pp. 8 (left), 13, and 18: Photos © Peter Kerze; p. 9: Photo © davidduncanlivingston.com; p. 12 (top): Photo © Jerry Gunnelson; p. 12 (bottom): Photo by Charles Bickford, courtesy Fine Homebuilding, © The Taunton Press, Inc.; pp. 14, 15, and 21: Photos © Sandy Agrafiotis; p. 16 (bottom): Photo © Carolyn L. Bates; p. 17: Photo © Audrey Hall; p. 19: Photo © Matthew Wilson; p. 20 (top): Photo © Amy Belding Brown.

The Rustic Cabin
pp. 22 and 23 (left): Photos © davidduncanlivingston.com.; p. 23 (right): Photo © Peter Kerze.

Start with a Life-Size Model (pp. 24-29) Designer: Deane Hillbrand, Log and Timber Framer, Route 1, Box 84, Sturgeon Lake, MN 55783; (218) 658-4370. Photos © davidduncanlivingston.com.

The Community Cabin (pp. 30-35) Photos © davidduncanlivingston.com.

A Family Tradition (pp. 36-41) Photos © Peter Kerze.

A Cabin of a Different Stripe (pp. 42-47) Photos © davidduncanlivingston.com.

Steps up a Hillside (pp. 48-53) Photos © Peter Kerze.

Big at Heart (pp. 54-59) Photos © davidduncanlivingston.com.

Maintaining Integrity (pp. 60-65) Photos © Randy O'Rourke, except top photo on p. 65 © Evan Sklar.

Rustic Oasis (pp. 66-71) Photos © davidduncanlivingston.com.

A Chain of Perfect Cabins (pp. 72-77) Architect: Edwin Lundie. Photos © davidduncanlivingston.com.

The Transformed Cabin
p. 78: Photo © Shaffer/Smith Photography; p. 79 (left): Photo © Charles Register; p. 79 (right): Photo © davidduncanlivingston.com.

Tobacco Barn to Log Cabin (pp. 80-85) Designer: Bernard Flippin, 6401 Fancy Gap Highway, Fancy Gap, VA 24328; (540) 728-2556. Photos © davidduncanlivingston.com.

A Clever Conversion (pp. 86-91) Architect: Chad Floyd with J. Whitney Huber (Centerbrook Architects and Planners), P. O. Box 955, Centerbrook, CT 06409; (860) 767-0175. Photos © Shaffer/Smith Photography.

Reviving a Ghost Town (pp. 92-97) Photos © davidduncanlivingston.com.

An Odd Couple (pp. 98-103) Architect: Marcel Breuer. Photos © Evan Sklar.

Rescuing a Heritage (pp. 104-109) Architect: Hearthstone Homes, 120 Carriage Drive, Macon, GA 31210; (912) 474-9370. Photos © Charles Register.

The Traditional Cabin
p. 110: Photo © Norman McGrath; p. 111 (left): Photo © davidduncanlivingston.com; p. 111 (right): Photo © Michael Jensen.

Ties to the Land (pp. 112-117) Architect: Geoffrey Prentiss (Prentiss Architects), 1218 6th Ave. W., Seattle, WA 98119; (206) 283-9930. Photos © davidduncanlivingston.com.

Log Cabin with a View (pp. 118-123) Architect: Jeremy Oury (Kibo Group Architecture, PC), 224 North Higgins, Ste. A, Missoula, MT 59802; (406) 542-5050. Photos © davidduncanlivingston.com.

More than the Sum of Its Parts (pp. 124-129) Architect: Kim Hoelting (Ross Chapin Architects), P. O. Box 230, Langley, WA 98260; (360) 221-2373. Photos © davidduncanlivingston.com.

Do-It-Yourself from a Kit (pp. 130-135) Designer: Shelter-Kit, Inc., 22 W. Mill St., Tilton, NH 03276; (603) 286-7611. Photos © Michael Jensen.

Cabin out Back (pp. 136-141) Architect: Annette Lindbergh (Tiny Houses, Inc.), 48 Peekskill Hollow Rd., Putnam Valley, NY 10579; (914) 526-4753. Photos © Rob Karosis.

Paradise on a Budget (pp. 142-147) Architect: Thomas Lawrence, Lawrence Architecture, 5512 1st Ave. NE, Seattle, WA 98105; (206) 332-1832. Photos © davidduncanlivingston.com.

Wilderness Wonderland (pp. 148-153) Architect: Jeff Sheldon (Prairie Wind Architecture), Box 626, Lewistown, MT 59457; (406) 538-2201. Photos © davidduncanlivingston.com.

The Better to See the Water (pp. 154-159) Architect: William Witt, 2000 Alaskan Way, Ste. 151, Seattle, WA 98121; (206) 441-1100. Photos © Michael Skott.

Like Living on a Yacht (pp. 160-165) Designer: Bruce Darring, P. O. Box 882, Saranac Lake, NY 12983; (518) 891-5943. Photos © Randy O'Rourke.

All You Really Need (pp. 166-171) Architect: Dale Mulfinger (SALA Architects, Inc.), 440 2nd St., Excelsior, MN 55331; (952) 380-4817. Photos © davidduncanlivingston.com.

Planning a Community (pp. 172-177) Architect: Rob Thallon and David Edrington, Thallon Architecture, 2303 McMorran St., Eugene, OR 97403; (541) 344-5201. Photos © John Anthony Rizzo.

A Better Place to Enjoy Nature (pp. 178-183) Architect: Mark Simon with Mahdad Saniee (Centerbrook Architects and Planners), P. O. Box 955, Essex, CT 06426; (860) 767-0175. Photos © Norman McGrath.

An Interim Strategy (pp. 184-189) Architect: Robert Knight, Knight & Associates, Architects, Beech Hill Rd., Blue Hill, ME 04614-0385; (207) 374-2845. Photos © Rob Karosis.

The Modern Cabin
pp. 190 and 191 (right): Photos © davidduncanlivingston.com; p. 191 (left): Photo © Randy O'Rourke.

Rocky Mountain Retreat (pp. 192-197) Architect: Ron Mason (Anderson Mason Dale Architects), 1615 17th St., Denver, CO 80202; (303) 294-9448. Photos © davidduncanlivingston.com.

Fresh Take on the Log Cabin (pp. 198-203) Architect: Thomas Blurock, Thomas Blurock Architects, 720 W. 17th St., Unit C, Costa Mesa, CA 92627; (949) 646-9373. Photos © Milroy and McAleer Photography.

Just for the Fun of It (pp. 204-207) Architect: James Stageberg, Stageberg Beyer Sachs Architects., Inc., 115 N. 4th St., Minneapolis, MN 55401; (612) 375-1399. Photos by Charles Bickford, courtesy Fine Homebuilding, © The Taunton Press, Inc.

Academic Freedom (pp. 208-213) Architect: Nick Winton (Anmahian Winton Architects), 147 Sherman St., Cambridge, MA 02140; (617) 497-6600. Photos © davidduncanlivingston.com.

Contemporary Dogtrot (pp. 214-219) Architect: Stephen Atkinson, Studio Atkinson, 85 Prescott St., #46, Cambridge, MA 02138; (617) 876-8892. Photos © Chipper Hatter.

A Cabin as Ship (pp. 220-225) Architect: Brian Mackay-Lyons Architecture, Halifax, Nova Scotia, Canada. Photos © davidduncanlivingston.com.

In Nature and of Nature (pp. 226-231) Seth Peterson Cottage Conservancy, Sand County Service Co., P. O. Box 409, Lake Dalton, WI 53940; (608) 254-6551. Photos © Randy O'Rourke.

The Call of Loons and Ospreys (pp. 232-237) Architect: Annie Ryan & Brian Meyer Studio, 589 Lincon Ave., St. Paul, MN 55102; (651) 290-0477. Photos © davidduncanlivingston.com.

Floating on a Wisconsin Prairie (pp. 238-243) Architect: Ralph Rapson (Ralph Rapson & Associates), 409 Cedar Ave. South, Minneapolis, MN 55454; (612) 333-4561. Photos © davidduncanlivingston.com.

A Salute to Frank Lloyd Wright (pp. 244-249) Designer: Frank Lloyd Wright. Photos © davidduncanlivingston.com.